THE COPING CODE

DR. KAMALJEET KAUR SIDDHU

Chennai • Bangalore

CLEVER FOX PUBLISHING
Chennai, India

Published by CLEVER FOX PUBLISHING 2025
Copyright © Dr.Kamaljeet Kaur Siddhu 2025

All Rights Reserved.
ISBN: 978-93-6709-48-5

This book has been published with all reasonable efforts taken to make the material error-free after the consent of the author. No part of this book shall be used, reproduced in any manner whatsoever without written permission from the author, except in the case of brief quotations embodied in critical articles and reviews.

The Author of this book is solely responsible and liable for its content including but not limited to the views, representations, descriptions, statements, information, opinions and references ["Content"]. The Content of this book shall not constitute or be construed or be deemed to reflect the opinion or expression of the Publisher or Editor. Neither the Publisher nor Editor endorse or approve the Content of this book or guarantee the reliability, accuracy or completeness of the Content published herein and do not make any representations or warranties of any kind, express or implied, including but not limited to the implied warranties of merchantability, fitness for a particular purpose. The Publisher and Editor shall not be liable whatsoever for any errors, omissions, whether such errors or omissions result from negligence, accident, or any other cause or claims for loss or damages of any kind, including without limitation, indirect or consequential loss or damage arising out of use, inability to use, or about the reliability, accuracy or sufficiency of the information contained in this book.

CONTENTS

Foreword .... *v*
Acknowledgments .... *xii*

1. The Coping Code: Coping With the Death of A Spouse 1
2. The Coping Code: Coping With Imprisonment 10
3. The Coping Code: Coping With the Death of A Close
   Family Member 13
4. The Coping Code: Coping With Personal Injury Or Illness 19
5. The Coping Code: Coping With Grief From Marriage
   With An Incompatible Spouse 26
6. The Coping Code: Coping With Grief From Dismissal
   From Work 33
7. The Coping Code: Coping With Grief From Retirement 39
8. The Coping Code: Coping With Grief From A Change
   in the Health of A Family Member 46
9. The Coping Code: Coping With Grief From Pregnancy
   Complications 53
10. The Coping Code: Coping With Grief From Business
    Readjustment 60
11. The Coping Code: Coping With Grief From A Change in
    Financial State 67
12. The Coping Code: Coping With Grief From A
    Major Mortgage 74

13. The Coping Code: Coping With Grief From Change in Responsibilities At Work 81
14. The Coping Code: Coping With Grief From A Child Leaving Home 88
15. The Coping Code: Coping With Grief Due to Trouble With in-Laws 95
16. The Coping Code: Coping With Grief Due to A Family Member's Suicide Attempt 102
17. The Coping Code: Coping With Grief Due to Failure in Examination Or Course 109
18. The Coping Code: Coping With Grief Due to Trouble With Your Boss 115
19. The Coping Code: Coping With Grief Due to Change in Working Hours Or Conditions 122
20. The Coping Code: Understanding and Preventing Suicide: Supporting Loved Ones Through the Darkest Times 129

Suicide Prevention Helpline... 137

FOREWORD

*I*n today's fast-paced world where emotional well-being often takes a backseat, **The Coping Code** by Dr. Kamaljeet Kaur stands out as an essential guide. This book delves deeply into human emotions uncovering their origins and offering effective management strategies. With a harmonious blend of empathy and scientific knowledge, Dr. Kaur provides not just insights but practical tools to navigate life's emotional turbulence. Whether you're grappling with anxiety, stress, or everyday ups and downs, **The Coping Code** empowers you to understand and master your emotions, paving the way for a healthier, more resilient life.

This insightful and inspiring book helps you prepare for success suggests ways to recover from setbacks, and achieve balanced, ongoing growth towards personal excellence. It bridges vision and action, providing leadership tools to leverage your time and talent, activate your faith, and make your vision a reality.

Dr. Sanjeev Rastogi
Ph(d), FCA, ACS, ACMA, B.Com Hons
CEO- Adani GCC, Adani Enterprise

Foreword

Many books have been authored on handling the human agony in the hours of crisis, however this book, authored by Dr. Kamaljeet is a special work to deal with personal rollercoaster which would enable self to manage the emotional and mental conditions at the time of an unforeseen and sudden negative change in life.

I know Dr Kamaljeet since last 15 years from the days when she was a young struggler who wishes to set the things right with a positive perspective. She, apart from her regular job, devotes herself for emancipation of human being form the negative atmosphere and encourages people to move on and fulfill the goal of living and helping others.

The book "COPING CODE" is not only a work of the Dr. Kamaljeet, but it intends to help and guide human beings when they face catastrophic changes in life and when one is not able to see way-out. The "Coping Code" will guide us to self-evaluate the situation at a time one is gloomy and no ray of hope is visible in life. Stepwise handling ourself in such situation has been aptly brought out in the book in a practical manner which is simple to comprehend and exercise.

To add to this, I would like to mention that the day I read the book, chapter -01, I could think of one of my friends, who retired recently from a Cent Govt job and lost her husband a month ago. Due to sudden demise of her husband, she is depressed and she is losing interest in everything she used to like. I gave her the write

Foreword

up to her to read and analyze her situation. She seems to be quite comfortable and trying to cope up the situation slowly.

I would congratulate Dr. Kamaljeet for writing this book, which I feel is not only a book but to address the social cause. This is a wonderful book which will be helpful to every human being since various situations brought out in the book is relevant to each one of us

My best wishes to the readers and the author of the book.

Mukul Gaur, IOFS
Dy Director General (Retd)
Govt of India, Ministry of Defence

In our rapidly changing and fast-paced world, stress has become a constant presence, appearing in countless ways—from the demands of work and personal relationships to the wider fears associated with societal pressures, events around us, changes in our lives, and various circumstances we navigate through. This book "The Coping Code" acts as a guiding light, providing readers with a thorough set of tools to help them steer through the chaotic aspects of contemporary life. Delving into different situations in our lives, the book provides amazing insights on dealing with various stresses we go through. Encouraging a path of self-discovery and emotional development, this book invites readers to turn stress from a formidable foe into a driving force to rediscover oneself and reimagine the stress differently.

DD Mishra
Research Vice President, Gartner

No one is immune to sadness, but in The Coping Code, Dr. Kamaljeet Kaur reveals how we can transform this emotion from a burden to a source of strength. This book demystifies sadness, showing it as a natural response to life's challenges, and provides practical advice on how to cope with it. With a focus on emotional resilience, Dr. Kaur's book will help readers face their struggles with a renewed sense of hope and understanding."

Mr. Aniruddha Deshpande
Managing Director, City Corporation Limited

In *The Coping Code*, Dr. Kamaljeet Kaur offers a roadmap to emotional growth, showing how sadness, though painful, can be an opportunity for personal transformation. This book empowers readers by offering practical tools for coping, while also encouraging them to embrace their emotions with understanding

Foreword

and kindness. Whether you're experiencing a difficult life event or simply facing the ups and downs of daily life, this book will help you cultivate the inner strength to face it all.

Dr. Sushant Patil,
Founder President Dr. D. Y. Patil Educational Federation, Varale, Talegaon Dabhade, Advisor to Ajeenkya D. Y. Patil Group

Life is not a straight line—it bends, breaks, and reshapes itself through moments of joy, despair, transition, and unexpected trials. What defines us is not whether we face challenges, but how we respond to them. In an era where mental health has rightly emerged from the shadows to become a critical conversation, *The Coping Code* by Dr. Kamaljeet Kaur Siddhu offers an indispensable resource for those navigating the complex terrain of grief, stress, and emotional upheaval.

This book is much more than a self-help guide—it is a lifeline, carefully crafted through years of counselling experience, emotional intelligence, and deep human insight. Dr. Siddhu addresses the unspoken truths that affect millions—bereavement, job loss, personal health crises, marital breakdowns, financial stress, and more—with clarity, sensitivity, and compassion.

Foreword

What makes *The Coping Code* truly exceptional is its structure. Every chapter is a standalone survival manual for a specific life event, backed by psychological research and real-life stories. Whether the reader is coping with the death of a loved one, the trauma of divorce, the stress of career transitions, or the silent sadness of empty-nest syndrome, this book offers practical strategies and comforting wisdom to help them move forward—not just to survive, but to rediscover meaning and purpose.

The strength of this book lies in its accessibility. Written in a warm, empathetic tone, it demystifies complex emotional reactions and normalizes the grieving process in its many forms. Readers are never judged here—only guided, encouraged, and empowered.

Moreover, the inclusion of global perspectives, tools like the Holmes and Rahe Stress Scale, and suicide prevention helpline information across countries makes this book not only relevant, but essential in our globally connected yet emotionally fragmented society.

The Coping Code is not only for those currently experiencing emotional hardship, but for anyone who wishes to build inner resilience, nurture emotional intelligence, and support others compassionately. It is equally valuable for mental health professionals, educators, caregivers, and community leaders who seek to make a real difference in the lives of those they serve.

Foreword

Dr. Kamaljeet Kaur Siddhu has created a book that will remain timeless in its relevance. Her work reminds us that grief and sadness are not detours—they are part of the human journey. With the right tools, support, and mindset, we can learn to cope, to rise, and to thrive.

Read this book slowly. Reflect on it deeply. And most importantly, pass it on—to someone who might need it more than they can say.

Mr. Anshul Sharma,
Founder Chairman
Shastri Group of Institutes, Pune.

ACKNOWLEDGMENTS

*A*s I embark on the journey of sharing *The Coping Code* with the world, I want to take a moment to express my heartfelt gratitude to the wonderful people who have been my unwavering support system throughout this endeavour.

First and foremost, I want to thank my dear husband, **Kripal Singh Siddhu**, whose love, encouragement, and patience have been a constant source of strength. To my amazing children, **Jessica** and **Montek Singh**, for inspiring me every day with their kindness and belief in me.

A special thank you to my parents, **Bishan Singh Real** and **Dharmi Devi Real**, whose love and wisdom have shaped the person I am today. I am also grateful to my mother-in-law, **Jaya,** for her blessings.

To my sister, **Manjeet Kaur Malhotra**, thank you for always being there with your words of encouragement and support.

To my elder brother, **Jagdish Singh Real and his wife Anuradha**, and to my younger brother, **Surjeet Singh Real and his wife Pinky**, who have all been my pillars of strength, never once letting me feel alone in this journey.

I would also like to acknowledge **Aditi Singh**, my wonderful executive assistant, whose dedication and persistence gave the

Acknowledgments

final push to make this book a reality. Without her, this project would have taken much longer to come to fruition.

My heartful thanks go to **Minu Rani** and **Sanat Deshpande**, my Toastmasters buddies, whose follow-ups and motivation were key in ensuring keeping me on track during the publication process.

This book would not have been possible without each of you. I am forever thankful for the love, encouragement, and belief you have all shown me. You have each played a vital part in helping bring *The Coping Code* into existence.

With love and gratitude,

Dr. Kamaljeet Kaur Siddhu

Warning:

Stress can cause severe health problems and, in extreme cases, death. While the stress-management techniques shared in this book have been shown to have a positive effect on reducing stress, they are for guidance only, and readers should take the advice of suitably qualified health professionals if they have any concerns over stress-related illnesses, or if stress is causing significant or persistent unhappiness. Health professionals should also be consulted before any major change in diet or levels of exercise.

THE COPING CODE

"The world breaks everyone, and afterward, some are strong at the broken places."
— Ernest Hemingway

Coping with Sad Feelings

Sadness doesn't have the power to dominate your day or your life. You have the power to manage your emotions and prevent them from lingering longer than necessary. Here are some healthy ways to cope with sadness and stress:

1. Acknowledge Your Feelings

The first step in dealing with sadness is to notice and accept it. Understand why you're feeling sad, but don't get stuck in it. It's okay to feel sadness—let it pass through you instead of letting it take over. Tell yourself, "I feel sad, but this too shall pass."

2. Bounce Back from Disappointments

Failure and disappointments are part of life, but they don't define you. If things don't go your way, don't give up. Learn from the experience and try again. Always remember: There's always a next time. A positive attitude can make all the difference.

3. Shift Your Perspective

Even when you're sad, try to find something positive to focus on. Think about your strengths, accomplishments, or what you can look forward to. A little bit of optimism can go a long way in changing your emotional outlook.

4. Seek Solutions

When facing a problem, focusing on possible solutions can help reduce feelings of helplessness. The act of problem-solving boosts self-confidence and helps you regain control over your emotions.

5. Reach Out for Support

Don't face your sadness alone. Talk to someone who cares—whether it's a friend, family member, or support group. Just sharing your feelings can help you feel lighter, and others may offer helpful perspectives or solutions.

6. Engage in Activities that Uplift You

Engage in activities that make you feel better—whether it's exercising, listening to music, creating art, or spending time with someone who makes you happy. It's easier to cope with sadness when you balance it with things that bring you joy.

Remember, dealing with sadness takes time and practice. By intentionally caring for your emotional health, you create space for happier feelings to emerge.

Comparing Yourself to Others: The Happiness Trap

It's natural to wonder, "Am I happy?" But measuring happiness is tricky. We often compare ourselves to others—our friends, colleagues, or even celebrities—and assume they're happier than we are. In reality, most people only show their positive emotions in public while concealing their struggles and sadness. This imbalance can make us feel like we're the only ones dealing with negative emotions, contributing to feelings of loneliness and dissatisfaction.

Research has shown that when we overestimate the happiness of others, we're more likely to feel isolated and dissatisfied. It's easy to fall into the trap of comparing ourselves to others, especially when we perceive them as "having it better." But remember: just because someone seems happy doesn't mean they are immune to grief, sadness, or stress.

A Comforting Thought

While it's easy to assume that others have it better, the truth is, they may be hiding their struggles. Media and art often portray sadness and grief in a way that reminds us we're not alone. Whether through movies, literature, or reality TV, seeing others express their emotions can be comforting, showing us that we're all in this together.

This book draws on years of research, including insights from the Holmes and Rahe Stress Scale, and the Life Events and Difficulties Schedule, tools used to measure the impact of life's challenges. Through personal training and counselling experiences, the author has observed patterns in how long sadness lasts after different life events. This book is designed to help you understand that while sadness is an inevitable part of life, its duration can be minimized. By recognizing the triggers of sadness and learning how to cope, you can move through difficult times more effectively and prevent unnecessary suffering.

Ultimately, **The Coping Code** offers a guide to understanding, processing, and reducing the impact of sadness, grief, and stress, empowering you to embrace life's challenges with resilience and hope.

THE COPING CODE: COPING WITH THE DEATH OF A SPOUSE

Maximum period of sadness: 12 months

> *"To love and be loved is to feel the sun from both sides."*
> *– David Viscott*

The loss of a spouse is one of life's most profound challenges. The sudden death of someone you've shared your life with is both devastating and disorienting. Anthony Paul, aged 52, experienced this loss when his wife, Rebecca, suddenly passed away at the age of 46. Rebecca had been his childhood sweetheart, his partner for 24 years. She was his everything—the light of his life. On one seemingly ordinary morning, she was fine, but by evening, she was gone. For Anthony, the grief was overwhelming. His life, which had revolved around Rebecca, was suddenly without her.

For a week, Anthony could not focus on anything. He was lost, struggling to understand how such an abrupt loss could have shattered his world. But instead of retreating further into isolation, he created a blog, *Lost Without Her*, and a forum for others to share their stories. Soon, Anthony discovered he wasn't alone in his grief. People shared stories of how they too were struggling with the death of a spouse, and others spoke of their journeys toward healing—through travel, new hobbies, and forming new relationships.

Through his research, Anthony learned that the grief following the death of a spouse is an immense emotional weight that can last anywhere from a few months to up to seven years. The depth of the grief depends largely on the nature of the relationship and the emotional bond shared. While it's impossible to predict how long grief will last, one thing is certain: you can find ways to cope with the loss and eventually create a fulfilling life again.

Losing a spouse is like being thrust into a completely new life. One moment you are married, and the next, you are navigating life as a single person—alone, with a heavy heart, and facing an uncertain future. Over time, the pain will likely subside, but the process of healing is gradual. Here are some strategies for coping with the grief of losing a spouse:

1. Go Easy on Yourself

Grief is a deeply personal experience, and there is no "right" way to grieve. Your emotional reaction depends on many factors—how long you were married, how your spouse passed, and your personal emotional resilience. It's normal to experience a range of emotions—shock, anger, sadness, and even guilt. You might feel guilty for still being alive or angry at your spouse for leaving you, or you might find yourself crying uncontrollably. Alternatively, you may feel numb or distant from the grief. What's important to remember is that your grief is unique, and there is no timeline for healing.

The people around you may not always know the best way to support you. They might offer clichés like "They're in a better place," or even avoid talking about your spouse, unsure of how to comfort you. If you feel ready, communicate your needs to your friends and family. Let them know if you want to talk about your spouse or if you need space. Be patient with others, as they too are navigating their own emotions.

2. Take Care of Your Physical Health

Grief takes a toll not only on your emotions but also on your physical well-being. The stress and emotional weight of loss can lead to a loss of appetite, trouble sleeping, or even physical pain. Taking care of your body during this time is crucial. Make an effort to eat balanced meals, exercise when you can, and prioritize rest. Avoid turning to substances like alcohol or overindulging in food to numb the pain—while it may seem comforting in the moment, it will only prolong your grief in the long run.

Research shows that the surviving spouse's health can decline during the early months of grieving, so it is essential to care for yourself physically as well as emotionally.

3. Seek Support

The pain of losing a spouse can be incredibly isolating. You may feel as though no one understands your unique loss, but reaching out for support is one of the most important things you can do for yourself. Studies suggest that a lack of social support is linked to prolonged depression and complicated grief. It's vital to surround yourself with people who care—family, friends, or even a therapist who can help you process your emotions.

You might also consider joining a support group for people who are grieving. These groups, either in person or online, can provide a sense of community and understanding. Knowing that others are experiencing the same grief can offer a comforting reminder that you are not alone.

4. Adjust Your Social Life

Navigating your social life after the death of a spouse can feel daunting. You might find it difficult to participate in social events where couples are present, or you may feel awkward when meeting friends who knew you as part of a couple. It's okay to say no to invitations or to let your friends know that you need some time alone or to spend time with people individually rather than in groups.

On the other hand, this can be a chance to rediscover yourself and make new connections. Consider joining a new class, taking up a hobby you've always wanted to try, or volunteering. Reaching out to new people or finding new activities can help you fill the void left by your spouse and start building new memories.

5. Seek Help for Complicated Grief

While grief is a natural response to loss, sometimes it can become overwhelming and prevent you from moving forward. This is known as "complicated grief," and it affects a significant percentage of those who have lost a spouse. If you are struggling to find meaning or purpose, experiencing prolonged feelings of guilt, or avoiding social interactions, you may be experiencing complicated grief.

If these feelings persist, it's important to reach out for professional help. A counsellor or therapist who specializes in grief can guide you through the healing process and offer strategies to help you cope. Sometimes, professional treatment is necessary to help you regain a sense of balance and hope.

A Final Thought

> *"Grief is not a sign of weakness, nor a lack of faith... It is the price of love."*
>
> **– Unknown**

Losing a spouse is an experience that changes you forever. It may take time—sometimes years—to come to terms with your loss, but it's possible to emerge from grief stronger and with a renewed sense of purpose. The memories of your spouse will always remain, and the love you shared will continue to shape your life, even as you move forward.

Through patience, self-care, and support from others, you will find your way back to living a fulfilling life, just as Anthony Paul did after the death of his beloved Rebecca.

THE COPING CODE: COPING WITH DIVORCE

Maximum period of sadness: 12 months

> *"Sometimes good things fall apart so better things can fall together."*
>
> **– Marilyn Monroe**

Divorce is one of the most difficult life transitions, especially when you have invested your heart and soul into the relationship. Elizabeth and Jack were once inseparable. In the early years of their marriage, they were like lovebirds, sharing dreams, laughter, and plans for a bright future. However, as Jack's business flourished, Elizabeth dedicated herself to raising their children, and gradually, their lives began to drift apart. Jack became involved with his secretary, and, under pressure, he chose to pursue a divorce, leaving Elizabeth devastated. For her, the sudden end of the relationship felt like a crushing blow, and she found herself overwhelmed with sadness, even contemplating ending her life.

Research shows that divorce is a life-changing event that can create a profound emotional response, sometimes taking anywhere from a few days to a few years to overcome, especially when one spouse is deeply committed to the relationship. In Elizabeth's case, her grief was amplified by the sense of betrayal and the loss of her family dynamic. But as hard as it is to imagine during the throes of grief, it is possible to heal, rebuild, and embrace a new future.

Here are some tips for overcoming the sadness and emotional turmoil of divorce:

1. Write a Goodbye Letter

One powerful way to process the emotions surrounding divorce is by writing a goodbye letter. Sit down with a pen and paper and express your farewell to the parts of your life that are now changing. Write about your role as a spouse, the traditions you shared, the dreams you had for the future, and the relationships that may have been altered—whether it's with your ex, in-laws, or friends who may not be there for you in the way you expected.

This letter may be painful, but it helps you face the reality of what you're losing and provides catharsis. It's a way to articulate your grief and understand what it is you need to heal from. By acknowledging these losses, you create space to begin moving forward.

2. Write a Hello Letter

After saying goodbye to what's behind, it's time to look ahead. Write a "hello" letter to the future, describing everything you're excited about now that you are no longer in the marriage. This might include rediscovering activities you once loved but had to set aside, the joy of having a peaceful night without disruption, or the newfound freedom to be yourself.

The hello letter is a tool for shifting your focus from grief to the possibilities of your new life. It reminds you of the positive changes that come with the end of a marriage and helps you begin to embrace the future. And don't stop after one letter—keep writing as new joys and opportunities come your way. Over time, the hello letter can serve as a roadmap for the life you're building.

3. Start Paying Attention to Your Inner Dialogue

Divorce often comes with a great deal of self-blame, guilt, and negative self-talk. You might find yourself questioning your worth or replaying the same hurtful thoughts over and over. It's crucial to begin recognizing and changing these internal conversations.

Instead of letting negative thoughts take over, try replacing them with positive affirmations. For example, call yourself resilient, strong, and capable. You're not just the sum of your past marriage; you are a whole person deserving of love and happiness. Shifting your internal dialogue can significantly help reduce feelings of inadequacy or shame and rebuild your sense of self-worth.

4. Get More Human Touch

A common aspect of divorce is the loss of physical intimacy—the hugs, the touch, the closeness. If you're feeling the absence of this contact, it's important to seek out healthy ways to fulfil that need. Schedule a massage, become known as the "hugger" in your social circle, or even treat yourself to a manicure or pedicure.

If the idea of hugging yourself seems silly, give it a try. Wrap your arms around yourself, hold the hug for a few moments, and focus on how it feels. It's a simple yet powerful way to comfort yourself and affirm your worth. This act of self-compassion can help you feel supported and loved, even in the absence of a partner.

5. Imagine Meeting Yourself One Year from Today

Take a moment to envision yourself one year from now. Picture a future where you're thriving—where you've moved beyond the pain and are living a full, rewarding life. What does that life look like? Where are you living? What are you doing for work? How are you feeling emotionally? Be as detailed as possible.

This exercise is about creating a vision for your future. By setting your sights on the positive changes that are possible in the coming year, you begin to take the first steps toward making that vision a reality. The more detailed your vision, the clearer the path becomes to achieving it.

A Final Thought

"The darkest hour has only sixty minutes."
– Morris Mandel

While it may seem impossible to imagine now, the sadness of divorce will not last forever. In time, your heart will heal, and you will rediscover joy in your life. Each of the steps outlined above—writing goodbye and hello letters, changing your internal dialogue, seeking physical comfort, and imagining a brighter future—is a way to help you move forward with grace and self-love.

Elizabeth's journey, though painful, can serve as a reminder that even after the most heartbreaking of separations, a fulfilling and vibrant life is waiting on the other side. The road to recovery may be long, but with each step, you'll grow stronger and more connected to the beautiful future that lies ahead.

THE COPING CODE: COPING WITH IMPRISONMENT

Maximum Period of Sadness: 9 Months

> "Out of suffering have emerged the strongest souls; the most massive characters are seared with scars."
>
> – Khalil Gibran

Imprisonment is a painful experience. It's an overwhelming sense of loss, disconnection, and fear. But even in the darkest of places, there is always a way to endure, learn, and eventually emerge stronger. This chapter offers tools to help you cope with the grief and trauma of being incarcerated.

Here are some essential tips for overcoming grief in prison:

1. Trust Your Instincts and Build Awareness

Living in a prison is like navigating a world of constant danger. Trust your gut, especially when you feel something isn't right. Whether it's a bad vibe from another inmate or the situation around you feel tense, act quickly to find a safe place. **Your first impressions are often your most accurate survival tool.**

Tip: If you sense danger, don't second-guess. Move fast, stay alert, and never ignore your instincts.

2. Respect Others, Stay Humble

Prison is a place where respect is hard-earned but invaluable. Live by the golden rule: **"Do unto others as you would have them do unto you."** Avoid confrontation, don't invade personal space, and keep your dignity. Respectful behaviour can prevent a lot of trouble.

Tip: Avoid insults, don't cut lines, and steer clear of unnecessary fights. This attitude will keep you safer and help you maintain your peace of mind.

3. Stay Mentally Active and Educate Yourself

Prison time can stretch on endlessly, but filling that time with meaningful activities can help ease the mental strain. Whether it's reading, taking classes, or exercising your brain, staying engaged keeps depression at bay.

Tip: Use your time to educate yourself. Take a GED class, learn a new skill, or read about something that interests you. The more you invest in yourself, the less you'll focus on the painful present.

4. Find Solace in Physical Health

Exercise is one of the most powerful tools for maintaining mental health. In prison, physical fitness can become your outlet. Regular exercise can reduce stress, elevate your mood, and help you feel more in control of your body and your environment.

Tip: Incorporate regular physical activity into your day, whether it's weightlifting, walking, or stretching. Physical strength can give you mental resilience as well.

5. Stay Connected to Family and Loved Ones

Your family remains your anchor in the chaos of incarceration. Despite the distance, maintaining communication with loved ones helps preserve your sense of identity and hope for the future. They are likely suffering too, so it's important to maintain strong emotional ties.

Tip: Write letters, make phone calls, and make the most of visits. Show gratitude for their support and keep the connection alive. Your role as a father, mother, or spouse doesn't end because you're in prison. Do your best to stay involved with their lives.

Surviving Prison Life: The Final Word

Surviving prison is not about simply enduring; it's about growing stronger amidst adversity. By trusting your instincts, respecting others, staying mentally and physically healthy, and staying connected to those who love you, you can begin to heal the emotional wounds and overcome the grief of imprisonment.

As you navigate this chapter of your life, remember that the scars you bear today can shape you into a stronger, more resilient person tomorrow. "Out of suffering have emerged the strongest souls…" As painful as this experience may be, it has the potential to be a transformative one. Keep moving forward.

THE COPING CODE: COPING WITH THE DEATH OF A CLOSE FAMILY MEMBER

Maximum Period of Sadness: 9 Months

"Grief is the price we pay for love."
– **Queen Elizabeth II**

Losing a loved one is one of the most profound and heartbreaking experiences we can endure. When death strikes, it feels like your world has been torn apart, leaving you with space that cannot be filled. Grief doesn't have a set timetable, and everyone experiences it in their way. Some find comfort in talking about their loss, while others retreat into silence. Some may want to process their feelings with others, while others prefer solitude. This chapter is dedicated to understanding the journey of grieving and learning how to heal, no matter how long it takes.

Anna's world turned upside down when her mother, Margaret, passed away suddenly from a heart attack. The shock left her numb, and for weeks, she struggled to process the reality of her loss. Margaret had been her confidante, her best friend, and now, the thought of life without her felt unbearable. Anna's house felt empty, each corner echoing with memories of her mother's laughter and warmth.

At first, Anna isolated herself. She couldn't bring herself to talk to anyone. Her grief felt too personal, too overwhelming to share. But after a couple of weeks, she realized she wasn't getting any better. Her physical health began to decline—she wasn't eating, she couldn't sleep, and she felt drained all the time.

One evening, her sister Sarah called. She gently encouraged Anna to join a grief support group. Reluctantly, Anna agreed, feeling as though she might gain some relief just by hearing others talk about their experiences. The first meeting was difficult, but as she listened to others share their stories, Anna felt a shift. She wasn't alone in her pain. Others understood exactly what she was going through.

Inspired by the support group, Anna began writing in a journal. It started as simple scribbles, but soon, she was pouring out her heart, recounting cherished memories of her mother. She also began keeping some of her mother's old scarves and books as mementos, items that provided comfort when she was overwhelmed.

As the months passed, Anna found a new sense of purpose. She joined a yoga class and started going on walks in the park, something her mother had always loved. Slowly, she returned to the things that made her happy, though her sadness still lingered. She even started a small garden in her mother's honour, planting her favourite flowers.

One year later, Anna held a small gathering with her family. Together, they shared stories of Margaret and planted a tree in her memory. It wasn't a "goodbye"—it was a way of honouring the love and lessons she had left behind. Anna still missed her mother deeply, but she had found a way to live with her grief, creating new traditions and holding on to her mother's memory in a healthy, healing way.

Tips for Overcoming Grief After the Loss of a Close Family Member

1. **Allow Yourself to Grieve:** It's important to remember that there's no "right" way to grieve. There's no manual for loss, and it's okay to feel a range of emotions, even when they seem contradictory. Grief can come in waves, sometimes sudden and overwhelming, and other times lingering quietly in the background. Allow yourself the space to grieve however you need to, without judgment.

Tip: Let yourself feel your emotions. Don't rush the process of healing, and know that grief doesn't follow a linear path.

2. **Take Care of Your Body:** Grieving can take a toll on your physical health, affecting your appetite, sleep, and energy levels. While it's difficult, try to maintain basic self-care routines. Eat nourishing meals, get outside for a walk, and aim to get enough sleep. Your body needs support, and the more you care for yourself physically, the more resilient you'll become emotionally.

Tip: Make time to rest, eat well, and get some exercise—even small steps can make a big difference in your well-being.

3. **Talk to Others:** Though grief can feel isolating, you don't have to go through it alone. Talk to friends, family members, or a counsellor. Expressing your feelings can lighten the emotional burden and help you make sense of the chaos that follows a loss. Remember that it's okay to ask for help.

Tip: Be specific when reaching out. Let others know what you need—whether it's someone to listen or someone to distract you.

4. **Join a Support Group:** Sometimes, it helps to talk to people who are going through similar experiences. Grief support groups can offer a safe space to share your feelings without fear of judgment. Whether in-person or online, connecting with others who understand can provide a sense of community during a lonely time.

Tip: Find a local or online grief support group to share your story and learn from others in similar situations.

5. **Keep Their Memory Alive**: The memory of your loved one may feel bittersweet, but holding onto those memories can be a crucial part of the healing process. Consider keeping meaningful belongings or doing something that honours their life, whether it's creating a memorial, planting a tree, or simply keeping a photo of them close.

Tip: Take time to hold on to meaningful objects or memories that remind you of your loved one. These can be comforting as you navigate your grief.

6. **Express Yourself Creatively**: Sometimes, words aren't enough to express the pain and complexity of grief. If you enjoy creative expression, try using art, writing, or music to process your emotions. Creating something meaningful out of the sadness can be incredibly therapeutic, and it can also serve as a tribute to the person you've lost.

Tip: Try journaling, painting, or creating a memory book. Art can provide an emotional outlet when words fail.

7. **Practice Self-Compassion**: During grief, you may feel guilt, anger, or frustration, and it's easy to turn these feelings inward. Be kind to yourself. Remind yourself that there's no "right" way to cope, and it's okay to not have everything figured out. Treat yourself with the same kindness and patience you would offer to a close friend.

Tip: Practice self-compassion. Permit yourself to feel however you need to and avoid self-criticism.

8. **Seek Spiritual Support**: If you are religious or spiritual, turn to your faith for comfort. Participate in rituals, seek solace in prayer or meditation, or talk to a spiritual leader. For some, these practices offer a sense of peace and connection that can help navigate the pain of loss.

Tip: Engage in spiritual or religious practices that bring you comfort. Take your time to explore your beliefs during this difficult time.

9. **Create New Traditions**: While it's important to honour old memories, part of healing after a loss involves creating new traditions. This may include celebrating holidays differently

or starting a new family ritual that brings comfort. Moving forward doesn't mean forgetting your loved one—it means finding a way to incorporate their memory into your life in a healthy, forward-looking way.

Tip: Start new traditions that honour your loved one while also helping you embrace the future. You can keep their memory alive in your everyday life.

10. **Seek Professional Help**: If you find that grief is overwhelming and interfering with your ability to function, it may be helpful to speak with a counsellor or therapist. Professional support can help you understand and constructively work through your grief, especially if you're experiencing complicated grief.

Tip: If your grief is persistent and disabling, consider seeking help from a trained therapist who specializes in grief counselling.

The Death of a Close Family Member leaves a gaping hole in your heart. But remember, grief is not something to "get over." It's an adjustment—a process of learning to live without the physical presence of your loved one. While the sadness may never fully disappear, it becomes something you can live with, something that evolves into a source of strength as you navigate the path to healing.

THE COPING CODE: COPING WITH PERSONAL INJURY OR ILLNESS

Maximum Period of Sadness: 9 Months

"The greatest glory in living lies not in never falling, but in rising every time we fall."

– **Nelson Mandela**

Dealing with a personal injury or illness can often feel like an emotional rollercoaster. Whether it's a sudden accident or the gradual onset of a chronic condition, the physical, emotional, and mental toll can leave you feeling overwhelmed and lost. However, healing—both physically and mentally—is possible. Grief, while not often talked about in the context of illness or injury, is very real. The sadness, frustration, anger, and fear that come with being hurt or sick are all part of the process. It's important to acknowledge those emotions and permit yourself to grieve. Healing takes time, and everyone's journey is different, but there are ways to manage the sadness and regain control of your life.

When Emily broke her leg in a car accident, her world was turned upside down. What began as a simple drive to the grocery store ended in an emergency room, with a shattered leg and a diagnosis of several months of recovery ahead. For the first few weeks, she was consumed by physical pain, and the emotional toll was even more severe.

She spent days in bed, feeling frustrated and isolated. She was used to being active—jogging every morning, attending yoga classes, and traveling on weekends—but suddenly, she couldn't even walk to the bathroom without crutches. The isolation and helplessness overwhelmed her.

Emily's friends and family visited often, but she pushed them away, feeling like a burden. "I don't want to be weak," she thought. "I just want to be myself again."

One afternoon, Emily's best friend, Laura, came to visit. She could see the sadness in Emily's eyes and gently encouraged her to speak with a counsellor. Laura shared how therapy had helped her in difficult times, and how Emily deserved the same kind of support.

At first, Emily resisted. But after several more weeks of emotional lows, she agreed to see a therapist. Talking through her feelings helped her realize that it wasn't weakness to seek help—it was a form of strength. The therapist helped her understand the grief she was experiencing, not only from the pain of her injury but also from the loss of the life she had known before.

Slowly, Emily began to make small changes. She allowed herself to rest and started accepting help from her family. She focused on what she *could* do—reading books she'd been meaning to get to, journaling about her thoughts, and finding comfort in daily routines. She even began learning mindfulness meditation to help calm her racing thoughts.

Over time, Emily's physical recovery progressed, but her emotional healing took longer. There were days when the sadness returned, but she no longer felt trapped by it. She learned to embrace the slower pace of life, finding gratitude in each small victory, whether it was a successful therapy session or the ability to walk short distances without assistance.

By the end of her recovery period, Emily was able to return to her active lifestyle, but she did so with a newfound appreciation for her body and mind. She no longer took her health for granted and had a deeper sense of compassion for herself. The road to healing wasn't linear, but Emily had learned the importance of patience, self-care, and asking for help along the way.

Tips for Overcoming Grief from Personal Injury or Illness

1. Acknowledge Your Emotions

It's easy to push emotions aside when dealing with physical pain or illness. However, it's essential to recognize and allow yourself to feel the sadness, frustration, anger, and even fear that accompany your condition. Bottling up emotions only prolongs the healing process.

Tip: Don't ignore your feelings. Take time to process the full range of emotions that come with an injury or illness.

2. Permit Yourself to Rest

The body and mind require rest in times of recovery. You might feel guilty about not being able to do everything you once could, but understand that healing requires time. Prioritize self-care and avoid pushing yourself too hard.

Tip: Rest is part of the healing process. Permit yourself to rest without guilt, and listen to your body's needs.

3. Focus on What You Can Control

Injuries or illnesses often leave you feeling helpless, but shifting your focus to the things you *can* control can help you regain a sense of empowerment. This might include managing your daily routine, choosing healthy foods, or practicing mindfulness.

Tip: Focus on what you can control, no matter how small. Setting small, achievable goals each day can help you regain a sense of control.

4. Build a Support System

Grief from an injury or illness often isolates us, but it's important to reach out to loved ones for support. Whether it's asking for help with everyday tasks or just having someone to talk to, a strong support system can make the healing process much easier.

Tip: Don't hesitate to lean on friends, family, or support groups. Sharing your feelings and experiences can ease the burden.

5. Consider Professional Therapy

If the emotional weight of your injury or illness becomes too much, it may help to talk to a therapist. Cognitive behavioural therapy (CBT) or counselling can be incredibly effective in helping you process your grief, reduce anxiety, and foster a sense of hope.

Tip: Therapy can offer valuable coping strategies. If needed, speak with a professional who specializes in grief and emotional well-being.

6. Accept Help When Offered

When you're facing a personal injury or illness, it's easy to become overwhelmed with the demands of daily life. Allow others to help, whether it's preparing meals, running errands, or providing emotional support.

Tip: Accept help when it's offered. Allowing others to assist you can relieve some of the emotional and physical stress you're experiencing.

7. Set Realistic Expectations

The recovery process is often slower than we want it to be. It's important to set realistic goals for your recovery and be patient with yourself. Progress may be slow, but every small improvement is a step toward healing.

Tip: Set small, realistic goals for yourself, and celebrate each milestone, no matter how minor it may seem.

8. Create a Routine

A sense of normalcy is key to healing. Create a daily routine that includes activities you enjoy, even if it's just a small hobby or a short walk outside. This can provide structure and a sense of accomplishment, even during difficult times.

Tip: Establish a routine to give your day structure and help ease feelings of chaos or uncertainty.

9. Practice Mindfulness or Meditation

The stress and anxiety that come with an illness or injury can be overwhelming. Mindfulness and meditation can help ground you in the present moment, reduce anxiety, and promote emotional healing. Take time each day to practice deep breathing or mindfulness exercises.

Tip: Try incorporating mindfulness or meditation into your daily routine. It can help reduce stress and promote emotional well-being.

10. Find Joy in the Small Moments

Even while recovering, it's important to find joy and peace in everyday experiences. Whether it's enjoying a quiet cup of coffee, spending time with a loved one, or watching a favourite show, seek out moments of joy, however small.

Tip: Look for the silver lining in each day. Even when life feels overwhelming, there are still moments to be thankful for.

Grief from a personal injury or illness is a unique and deeply personal experience. It requires patience, self-compassion, and a willingness to accept help when needed. Healing—both physically and emotionally—takes time, but with the right strategies and support, it is possible to rise above the sadness and find strength in the process.

THE COPING CODE: COPING WITH GRIEF FROM MARRIAGE WITH AN INCOMPATIBLE SPOUSE

Maximum Period of Sadness: 9 months

"The best way out is always through."
— **Robert Frost**

Marriage is often seen as a union built on love, trust, and shared goals. But sometimes, despite our best intentions, we find ourselves in a relationship with someone who feels incompatible, whether due to differences in values, emotional needs, or life goals. The grief that comes from being in a marriage with an incompatible spouse is often overlooked, but it is very real. The sadness, frustration, and emotional exhaustion can make every day feel like a struggle. However, even in these situations, there is hope for healing and self-growth. You can navigate through this grief with the right mindset, strategies, and self-care.

While the journey is difficult, the key is to allow yourself time to grieve, but also to understand that healing is not only possible—it is essential. Here are 10 important tips for overcoming the grief of being in a marriage with an incompatible spouse.

Rachel had been married to Daniel for eight years. On the surface, they appeared to have everything—two kids, a lovely house, and seemingly a happy life. But deep down, Rachel knew that their marriage was no longer fulfilling. Their values, once so aligned, had diverged over the years. Daniel's priorities were centred around his career and social life, while Rachel craved emotional intimacy and connection. They rarely spent quality time together, and when they did, they struggled to communicate effectively.

At first, Rachel tried to hold onto the hope that things would get better, that maybe Daniel would change, or that their relationship would return to how it had been when they first fell in love. But the years of unaddressed issues had taken their toll. Rachel found herself feeling emotionally exhausted and lonely. She grieved the relationship she had hoped for, the marriage she thought would bring mutual happiness.

One night, after another argument about their lack of connection, Rachel found herself crying for hours. She realized that she could no longer ignore the grief she was feeling—the grief for the marriage that never turned out the way she had envisioned, and the grief for the emotional distance between her and Daniel. She knew something had to change.

Rachel decided to seek therapy, not just individually but also as a couple. She learned that, while Daniel was unwilling to make any significant changes in their relationship, she was at a crossroads. She could either continue enduring the emotional pain or she could choose to move forward.

Through her therapy sessions, Rachel began to rebuild her sense of self. She remembered her passions and interests that had taken a backseat during her marriage. She spent more time with friends, began pursuing hobbies again, and focused on her children. Slowly, she started to heal. The sadness didn't disappear overnight, but with time, Rachel realized that she could live a full and happy life, whether or not her marriage worked out.

In the end, after much contemplation and difficult conversations with Daniel, Rachel made the painful decision to separate. It wasn't an easy choice, but it was the right one for her emotional and mental well-being. The grief was profound, but it also marked the beginning of a new chapter in her life. She had learned to prioritize her happiness, and over time, she found peace with her decision.

Tips for Overcoming Grief from Marriage with an Incompatible Spouse

1. Acknowledge Your Grief

Grief from a challenging marriage may not feel as tangible as other types of loss, but it is just as valid. Recognize that feeling sadness, frustration, or even anger in such a situation is normal. It's essential to let yourself process these emotions rather than pushing them down.

Tip: Allow yourself to feel and express your emotions without judgment. Grieving the loss of what you hoped your marriage would be is part of the healing process.

2. Accept the Reality of the Situation

It can be tempting to hold onto hope that things will magically improve or that your spouse will change. But accepting the reality that you are in an incompatible relationship is the first step toward healing. This acceptance does not mean giving up, but rather acknowledging the truth of your situation.

Tip: Take a step back and assess the reality of your relationship. Accepting where you are can help you move forward healthily.

3. Set Boundaries

When dealing with incompatibility in a marriage, it's important to establish healthy boundaries with your spouse. This might involve setting limits on conversations, emotional demands, or personal space. Boundaries help protect your emotional well-being.

Tip: Establish boundaries that protect your mental health and ensure you are not continually drained by the relationship dynamics.

4. Communicate Openly

Effective communication is key to any relationship, but especially in one with incompatibilities. Rather than allowing resentment or frustration to fester, try to express your thoughts and feelings calmly and respectfully. If direct communication feels impossible, consider marriage counselling to help facilitate these conversations.

Tip: Be open and honest about your feelings, but do so in a way that fosters understanding and cooperation.

5. Prioritize Self-Care

In difficult relationships, it's easy to lose sight of your own needs. Make sure you are taking care of your physical, emotional, and mental health. Engage in activities that bring you joy, and prioritize self-care as an essential part of healing.

Tip: Focus on your well-being by making time for activities that recharge you—whether it's exercise, hobbies, spending time with loved ones, or simply taking a break.

6. Seek Support

Going through grief from an incompatible marriage can feel isolating, but you don't have to go through it alone. Lean on trusted friends, family, or a therapist who can provide emotional support and offer different perspectives on your situation.

Tip: Find a support system that understands your struggles and can help guide you through the healing process.

7. Reflect on What You Need

Take time to reflect on your own emotional needs and desires. What are the qualities and values you want in a partnership? Understanding what you truly need from a relationship will help you make informed decisions about how to move forward.

Tip: Reflect on your emotional needs and whether they are being met in the relationship. This clarity will guide your choices going forward.

8. Consider the Possibility of Change

While an incompatible spouse may not change overnight, it's important to assess whether both of you are willing to work on the relationship. If both partners are committed to personal growth and improving the marriage, it may be possible to overcome incompatibilities through effort and compromise.

Tip: Consider whether both partners are open to change. If the willingness is there, working together with a therapist might help address issues in the marriage.

9. Learn from the Experience

Even in the most painful situations, there are lessons to be learned. Reflect on what the relationship has taught you about yourself, your values, and your desires. Use these insights to grow as an individual and to guide future relationship choices.

Tip: Take the lessons from the experience and use them to become stronger and more self-aware.

10. Make the Decision to Move Forward

Healing can only occur when you make the decision to either work on the relationship or to move forward. Recognizing when the relationship is no longer serving you and accepting that it's time to let go can be incredibly empowering. This might be a difficult choice, but it's an important step toward healing and personal growth.

Tip: Whether it's working through the issues or choosing to part ways, make the decision that is best for your mental health and future happiness.

Grief from an incompatible marriage is a long and painful process, but it doesn't have to define your life. By acknowledging the grief, taking care of yourself, and seeking the support you need, you can navigate through the sadness and come out stronger on the other side. The journey may be challenging, but healing and self-discovery are possible, and they can lead you to a brighter future.

THE COPING CODE: COPING WITH GRIEF FROM DISMISSAL FROM WORK

Maximum Period of Sadness: 6 months

> *"Success is not final, failure is not fatal: It is the courage to continue that counts."*
>
> – **Winston Churchill**

Losing a job can feel like a significant blow to your identity, self-worth, and sense of stability. Whether it's the result of downsizing, performance issues, or a mismatch between you and the company culture, being dismissed from work can leave you feeling defeated, uncertain, and grief-stricken. It's a type of grief that often goes unspoken but can be just as intense as losing a loved one. Just like any loss, it can bring with it denial, anger, depression, bargaining, and eventually acceptance. Healing is possible, and the road to recovery starts with acknowledging the sadness but refusing to let it define your future.

Tom had worked at a marketing firm for nearly six years. He had worked his way up, but recently, he'd noticed changes within the company—new leadership, shifting priorities, and tighter budgets. One day, during a meeting, his boss called him in and informed him that his position had been eliminated. The company was downsizing, and unfortunately, his department was no longer needed.

The news hit Tom like a freight train. He had invested so much of his time and energy into the company, believing that his job was secure. At first, he was in disbelief, then anger, followed by a period of depression. He spent the next few days feeling lost, unsure of what to do next. The job he had loved for so long was gone, and he wasn't sure where to go from here.

For the first few days, Tom allowed himself to grieve. He felt sad, frustrated, and anxious about the future. He took time off from his usual routine, trying to understand why this had happened. But as time passed, Tom started to reflect on his career. He realized that the job he had been doing no longer fulfilled him as it once did. The passion he once had for his work had slowly faded, and the company he worked for no longer aligned with his values.

Instead of dwelling on the loss, Tom used this setback as an opportunity for reinvention. He updated his resume, sought advice from former colleagues, and began networking. He also took some online courses to improve his digital marketing skills, which he knew would make him more competitive in the job market. Slowly, he began to regain his confidence.

A few months later, Tom landed a new position at a smaller company where he felt his skills were truly valued. His new role was in a much more dynamic environment, and he was working on projects that excited him again. While the grief from losing his old job never fully went away, Tom had used the experience to discover a path that was far more rewarding than he could have ever anticipated.

Here are **important tips** to help you overcome the grief of being dismissed from work and start rebuilding your confidence, your career, and your life.

Tips for Overcoming Grief from Job Loss

1. Allow Yourself Time to Grieve

It's natural to feel a range of emotions when you lose your job. The first step is to give yourself permission to grieve. Whether you feel anger, frustration, or sadness, don't rush the process. Take time to understand your emotions and feel them fully.

Tip: Take a few days off to process the shock of the dismissal. Don't feel guilty for taking this time for yourself. It's necessary for healing.

2. Don't Internalize the Loss

It's easy to take job loss personally, especially if it's due to performance or a personality conflict. However, remember that your job does not define you. The reasons for dismissal are not always a reflection of your worth as a person or a professional.

Tip: Separate your identity from your career. Understand that your value goes beyond the job you did.

3. Reframe the Situation

While being fired or let go can feel like an end, it may also be an opportunity for a new beginning. Reflect on whether the job was truly a good fit for you and whether it aligns with your passions and goals.

Tip: Ask yourself if this dismissal might be a nudge to explore new, more fulfilling opportunities. View this setback as a potential redirection rather than a failure.

4. Build a Support Network

Losing a job can feel isolating, but you don't have to go through it alone. Reach out to friends, family, or even professional networks who can offer emotional support and job-search guidance. Isolation will only prolong your grief.

Tip: Talk openly about your job loss. Sometimes, just voicing your feelings can provide relief, and others may offer valuable insights or opportunities you hadn't considered.

5. Refine Your Resume and Personal Brand

A dismissal doesn't mean you are not qualified or capable—it just means that particular job was not the right fit. Take this time to update your resume, LinkedIn profile, and personal brand to better reflect your skills, accomplishments, and future aspirations.

Tip: Focus on what you learned in your previous job, including any skills and positive contributions. Use these insights to frame your experience positively when seeking new employment.

6. Take Care of Your Mental Health

Unemployment can trigger anxiety, depression, and stress, especially if financial concerns come into play. It's vital to prioritize your mental well-being during this time. Practice relaxation techniques, engage in hobbies, and consider speaking to a therapist if necessary.

Tip: Schedule daily relaxation activities such as yoga, meditation, or even a simple walk to help manage stress. Keeping your mind clear will help you approach your job search with more clarity and confidence.

7. Expand Your Skills

Being out of work provides a unique opportunity to invest in yourself. Consider taking online courses, workshops, or certifications that could make you more marketable and open new career doors.

Tip: Learn something new that not only enhances your professional qualifications but also reignites your passion for your work. You may discover a new career path entirely.

8. Network and Stay Connected

Most job opportunities are found through networking, so don't shy away from reaching out to people you know in the industry. Attend networking events, connect with past colleagues, and make use of social media platforms like LinkedIn.

Tip: Be proactive in your networking. Attend job fairs, industry conferences, or join online communities where you can connect with others and learn about potential openings.

9. Reframe the Job Search as a New Challenge

The job hunt can be daunting, but it can also be an exciting challenge. Instead of viewing it as a burden, see it as a new chapter in your career journey. Approach each interview and application with a fresh perspective.

Tip: Create a structured job search plan with daily goals. Break down the process into manageable steps and celebrate small victories along the way.

10. Stay Positive and Patient

Job loss often doesn't lead to immediate results. It can take time to find the right opportunity. Remember that setbacks are part of the process, and patience is crucial. Stay positive, and trust that the right opportunity will come along.

Tip: Maintain a positive attitude, even when things seem tough. Reframe negative thoughts and focus on what you can control—your effort, you're learning, and your resilience.

Dismissal from work can shake you to your core, but with the right mindset, it can also be an opportunity for growth. By allowing yourself time to grieve, reframing the situation, seeking support, and staying proactive, you can emerge from the experience stronger and ready for new opportunities. Keep in mind that your career is not defined by a single setback—it's shaped by your resilience and ability to bounce back.

THE COPING CODE: COPING WITH GRIEF FROM RETIREMENT

Maximum Period of Sadness: 6 Months

"Don't cry because it's over, smile because it happened."
– Dr. Seuss

Retirement, while often seen as a long-awaited and exciting milestone, can also bring feelings of sadness, loss, and uncertainty. After years of dedicating your time to a career, stepping away from it can leave a void. It's common to experience grief, not just from leaving your job but also from the identity and routine it provided. The transition to retirement can feel like the end of a chapter, and with that comes a period of adjustment.

Margaret had worked as a teacher for over 40 years. Her days were filled with lesson plans, grading papers, and shaping the minds of young students. Her classroom was more than just a job to her—it was her life, her identity, and her purpose. So, when the day came for her to retire, she was excited for the possibilities of a new chapter, but she couldn't help but feel a deep sense of loss.

At first, Margaret tried to stay upbeat, telling herself that retirement would give her more time to travel, pursue hobbies, and relax. But, after the initial excitement wore off, she found herself feeling aimless and lonely. Her days no longer had the structure they once did, and she struggled to fill the hours that had once been occupied by students and colleagues. She missed the interaction, the sense of purpose, and the knowledge that she was making a difference in the world.

For the first few months, Margaret felt a profound sadness. She found herself reminiscing about the classroom, feeling disconnected from her sense of identity. It seemed like a strange and difficult transition, and she couldn't shake the feeling that something was missing. But, instead of sinking deeper into her grief, Margaret began following some advice she had read about coping with retirement.

First, she acknowledged her feelings. Margaret gave herself permission to miss her old life and the meaningful work she had done. She spent time journaling and reflecting on what she missed most about teaching.

Then, she decided to shift her focus toward finding a new purpose. Margaret had always enjoyed gardening, but she had never had the time to truly dive into it. She took a gardening course at a local community centre and soon became obsessed with learning about different plants and landscaping techniques. The hobby not only gave her a sense of accomplishment but also connected her with a new community of people who shared her interest.

Margaret also made sure to stay active. She joined a walking group, which helped her stay physically healthy and gave her a social outlet. She reconnected with former colleagues and started a book club with some friends. Slowly but surely, Margaret began to feel that her life still had meaning and excitement, just in a different way.

Six months into her retirement, Margaret was no longer filled with sadness. She had found new passions, new people, and a new sense of purpose. The grief had faded, replaced by an appreciation for the freedom and opportunities retirement had brought. While she would always cherish her time as a teacher, she had learned to embrace the new chapter in her life.

The good news is that the sadness associated with retirement is temporary. Research suggests that it typically takes about six months to adjust to this new phase of life. In the meantime, there are practical steps you can take to manage the emotional upheaval and make the most of this transition. Here are **important tips** to help you cope with the grief of retirement and move forward into this exciting new chapter.

Tips for Overcoming Grief from Retirement

1. Acknowledge Your Emotions

It's normal to feel a mixture of emotions when you retire, including sadness, anxiety, and even guilt. Allow yourself to feel these emotions without judgment. It's important to recognize that retirement is a huge life change, and it's okay to grieve the loss of your work life.

Tip: Take time to reflect on what you're feeling. Journaling or talking to someone close to you can help process your emotions.

2. Focus on the Positive Aspects of Retirement

While it's easy to focus on what you're losing, remember to look at the benefits. Retirement offers you more time for hobbies, travel, family, and relaxation. Embrace the freedom to explore passions or interests that may have been sidelined during your working years.

Tip: Make a list of the exciting opportunities you can now pursue. This can help you shift your perspective from loss to possibility.

3. Set New Goals

Retirement doesn't mean the end of goals; it's just the beginning of new ones. Setting goals can provide you with a sense of purpose and direction. Whether it's learning a new skill, writing a book, or volunteering, having something to look forward to can ease the sadness and give you a sense of accomplishment.

Tip: Create a "bucket list" of things you want to do during retirement. This can give you a fresh outlook on what you want to achieve in this new stage of life.

4. Establish a Routine

One of the biggest challenges in retirement is the lack of structure. A regular routine can help create a sense of normalcy and stability. Include activities that make you feel productive and fulfilled, whether it's exercising, gardening, or cooking.

Tip: Try to wake up at the same time each day and schedule activities that bring you joy. Creating structure can ease feelings of aimlessness.

5. Find a New Sense of Purpose

Work often provides a deep sense of purpose. Without it, you may feel lost or unsure of your place in the world. Finding new ways to contribute—whether through volunteering, mentoring, or working part-time—can help you regain that sense of purpose.

Tip: Explore volunteer opportunities in areas you're passionate about. Giving back can make you feel needed and valued, which is essential for maintaining your self-worth.

6. Nurture Relationships

Retirement can sometimes lead to feelings of isolation, especially if your social interactions were primarily work-related. It's essential to nurture relationships with family, friends, and old colleagues. Socializing and staying connected will help alleviate loneliness and provide emotional support during the transition.

Tip: Schedule regular meet-ups with friends and family, or join social groups and clubs to stay connected to others.

7. Stay Active and Healthy

Physical activity plays a significant role in emotional well-being. Regular exercise boosts your mood, reduces anxiety, and helps you stay healthy. Retirement is a great time to focus on your physical health—whether it's walking, yoga, swimming, or even joining a sports league.

Tip: Make exercise a daily habit. Not only will it improve your physical health, but it will also enhance your mood and help you feel more energized.

8. Explore New Hobbies

Retirement gives you the gift of time to discover new hobbies or revisit old ones. Whether it's painting, learning a musical instrument, or hiking, exploring new activities can bring joy and satisfaction to your life. It can also be a great way to meet new people and expand your social network.

Tip: Experiment with different hobbies and see which ones bring you the most joy. Don't be afraid to try something completely new.

9. Embrace Flexibility

Retirement is about freedom, and with that comes flexibility. This is your chance to explore different ways of living that weren't possible when you had a full-time job. Embrace the change and give yourself permission to slow down or take spontaneous adventures.

Tip: Try to let go of rigid expectations. If you want to spend a day doing nothing or travel at the last minute, embrace it. Flexibility will keep you feeling free and positive.

10. Seek Professional Help if Needed

If you find that your sadness or grief is prolonged or overwhelming, consider speaking to a therapist or counsellor. Transitioning into retirement can be a complex emotional process, and having a professional guide you through this period can be incredibly helpful.

Tip: If your grief extends beyond six months or you experience signs of depression, don't hesitate to seek professional support. Talking to someone can offer clarity and help you process your feelings.

Retirement can indeed be a difficult transition, but it also offers the chance for reinvention and growth. By allowing yourself to grieve the loss of your career, exploring new opportunities, and taking care of your emotional and physical health, you can make the most of this exciting new phase of life. Remember, retirement is not an end—it's a new beginning.

THE COPING CODE: COPING WITH GRIEF FROM A CHANGE IN THE HEALTH OF A FAMILY MEMBER

Maximum Period of Sadness: Until Family Member Recovers

> *"When you are sorrowful, look again in your heart, and you shall see that in truth you are weeping for that which has been your delight."*
>
> – Kahlil Gibran

The health of a family member is one of the most deeply personal and challenging aspects of life. Whether it's a sudden illness or a gradual decline, the news can shake you to your core. As a loved one, you naturally feel sadness, fear, and uncertainty. It's difficult to see someone you care about in pain or facing health challenges, and the emotional toll can be overwhelming. You may experience grief, even if the illness or health change doesn't involve death. The process of watching someone close to you struggle with health issues can trigger feelings of helplessness and sorrow.

However, the maximum period of sadness often correlates with the duration of their recovery. Once the family member recovers, so too will the weight of the sadness you feel. While it's a difficult journey, there are ways to cope and support both your loved one and yourself during this challenging time.

Sophia had always been the rock of her family. As the eldest daughter, she was the one who coordinated family gatherings, looked after her younger siblings, and ensured that everything ran smoothly. Her mother, Maria, had always been a vibrant and healthy woman—an active part of her community and a passionate cook who could whip up a meal that felt like home to everyone. So, when Maria suddenly fell ill with a chronic condition that affected her mobility and energy levels, it left Sophia and the entire family reeling.

At first, Sophia couldn't believe what was happening. She felt like her world had shifted overnight. Her mother, the pillar of strength in their family, was now dependent on others for basic tasks. Sophia was filled with fear and sadness, watching her mother struggle with her new reality. It was hard to accept that this vibrant woman, who had been so full of life, was now grappling with limitations she had never faced before.

For the first few weeks, Sophia threw herself into helping care for her mother. She took over many of her mother's responsibilities, such as cooking meals and running errands. But the constant worry and sadness started to take a toll on her. She was emotionally drained, and she realized she needed to take care of herself if she was going to be able to help her mom.

Sophia followed the advice she had heard about coping with such grief. First, she acknowledged her sadness. She allowed herself to cry and feel frustrated, but she also made time for quiet moments of self-reflection. She then sought support from her friends, talking openly about her fears and frustrations.

Instead of feeling powerless, Sophia started to focus on what she could control. She educated herself about her mother's illness and reached out to support groups for families of people with similar health conditions. This knowledge helped her to feel more empowered and gave her ideas on how to help her mother in practical ways.

Throughout the process, Sophia made sure she didn't neglect her own emotional and physical health. She found solace in taking short walks each day and made time for a weekly coffee date with a close friend to talk about her challenges. She also reached out to family members to share the responsibility of caregiving. By not trying to shoulder it all alone, she was able to prevent burnout and maintain her emotional well-being.

As the weeks passed, Sophia began to see small improvements in her mother's condition. Maria was able to regain some strength and independence, and Sophia found comfort in the progress, no matter how slow. The grief she felt lessened as she saw her mother recovering bit by bit, and eventually, the sadness she had initially felt gave way to a quiet sense of hope.

Sophia learned that while the journey was difficult, her emotional resilience and the support of her loved ones helped her through the hardest moments. Her mother's recovery wasn't just about physical healing—it was about the emotional healing of their entire family, and Sophia knew that they would get through it together.

In this chapter, we'll explore **tips** to help you manage the grief caused by a family member's health change, and ensure that you can navigate this period with strength and compassion.

Tips for Coping with Grief from a Change in the Health of a Family Member

1. Acknowledge Your Feelings

Grief is not just about death. It's about witnessing someone you love suffer and feeling helpless. Recognize your emotions—whether it's sadness, fear, anger, or frustration. These feelings are valid and part of the healing process.

Tip: Give yourself permission to feel. Talking about your emotions with someone you trust can help you process them.

2. Focus on What You Can Control

It's easy to become overwhelmed by the situation. However, focus on the things you can control. Perhaps it's offering your support in practical ways—helping with household chores, cooking meals, or providing transportation to doctor's appointments. These actions can make you feel like you're doing something positive.

Tip: Identify small, actionable ways you can assist your loved one. A simple, supportive gesture can make a big difference.

3. Take Care of Yourself

It's essential to look after your own well-being during times of stress. Caring for someone else can be physically and emotionally draining. Make sure you're getting enough rest, eating well, and engaging in activities that rejuvenate you.

Tip: Schedule time for self-care, even if it's just for a walk, a good book, or a quiet moment of reflection. You cannot support someone else if you are not taking care of yourself.

4. Provide Emotional Support, But Don't Neglect Your Own Needs

Sometimes, in the face of a loved one's illness, you might forget to check in with your own emotional needs. It's crucial to balance offering emotional support to your family member while also seeking support for yourself.

Tip: Find someone you can talk to about your feelings, whether it's a close friend, therapist, or support group. Sharing your concerns can help relieve some emotional strain.

5. Stay Positive, But Be Realistic

While it's important to remain hopeful, it's equally important to stay grounded in reality. Understand that recovery may be slow and filled with ups and downs. Positive thinking can help, but make sure your expectations align with the actual situation.

Tip: Focus on small victories and progress. Celebrate each step toward recovery, no matter how small.

6. Reach Out for Help

Don't be afraid to ask for help. Family members, friends, and even professionals can provide crucial support during this time. Whether it's emotional support or practical assistance, remember that you don't have to go through this alone.

Tip: Let others know how they can assist you—whether it's running errands or providing a listening ear.

7. Be Present

Sometimes the best thing you can do for a loved one who is ill is simply to be there for them. Sitting with them, holding their hand, or just being present can be a powerful act of love and support.

Tip: Avoid feeling pressured to "fix" the situation. Your presence, compassion, and patience are often the most helpful things you can offer.

8. Learn About the Illness

Educating yourself about your family member's condition can help you feel more empowered. Understanding the illness, its treatment, and the expected recovery timeline allows you to better support them and manage your expectations.

Tip: Research the illness, talk to healthcare providers, and join online communities where you can gain insights from others going through similar experiences.

9. Maintain a Routine

A health crisis can disrupt daily life, but maintaining some form of routine can provide a sense of normalcy and stability. Try to stick to regular schedules for meals, sleep, and activities that bring comfort, even if it's just in small ways.

Tip: Keep small routines intact, like having meals together or taking regular breaks for relaxation. Structure will help create a sense of stability.

10. Find Support Through Others in Similar Situations

Many people go through similar experiences and find it helpful to connect with others in the same boat. Whether through support groups, online forums, or community organizations, connecting with others who understand can make a big difference.

Tip: Seek out a support group or a network of people going through similar situations. Sometimes the best advice comes from those who've walked the same path.

When a family member faces health challenges, the emotional toll is significant. However, by acknowledging your grief, taking care of yourself, reaching out for support, and focusing on the positive steps toward recovery, you can navigate this challenging time with strength. Remember, your emotional healing often goes hand in hand with your loved one's recovery, and together, you can create a new chapter filled with hope and resilience.

THE COPING CODE: COPING WITH GRIEF FROM PREGNANCY COMPLICATIONS

Maximum Period of Sadness: 5 Months

> *"Grief is not a sign of weakness, nor a lack of faith. It is the price of love."*
>
> **– Anonymous**

Pregnancy is often a time filled with excitement and anticipation, but when complications arise, it can lead to feelings of fear, sadness, and uncertainty. The news of complications during pregnancy can shake you deeply, and navigating through this emotional journey can feel overwhelming. Whether it's the loss of a pregnancy, complications that threaten the health of the baby, or ongoing medical challenges for the mother, the grief felt during this time is real and deserves attention.

It's important to recognize that the sadness from pregnancy complications is valid. The emotional toll can be significant, but with support, self-compassion, and a focus on healing, the grief can be managed. While every experience is unique, the maximum period of sadness often correlates with the time it takes for the pregnancy complications to be resolved or the health of the baby and mother to stabilize.

Sarah had always dreamed of becoming a mother. She and her husband, Tom, had been trying for months to conceive, and when she finally saw the two pink lines on the test, it was one of the happiest moments of her life. The early months of her pregnancy were filled with excitement as she and Tom picked out baby names and imagined their future as a family. However, at her 12-week ultrasound, Sarah's excitement was met with fear when the doctor discovered complications.

The doctor explained that there was a risk to both Sarah and the baby, and they would need to monitor the situation closely. Sarah was devastated. The uncertainty about the health of her baby caused a deep sadness that lingered for weeks. She felt a sense of helplessness that she had never known before. Each doctor's appointment seemed to bring more questions than answers, and the emotional toll on Sarah was heavy.

At first, Sarah tried to stay strong, but the sadness and fear consumed her. She withdrew from friends and family, not wanting to talk about the pain she felt. It wasn't until a close friend reached out to her that she began to realize she couldn't face this alone. Her friend encouraged her to talk to Tom about her feelings, and together, they began to navigate the emotional rollercoaster of the pregnancy complications.

Sarah took time to grieve the loss of the pregnancy she had envisioned. She allowed herself to cry and express her frustration, but she also sought knowledge. She researched the complications and attended support groups for other women going through similar experiences. As she learned more about her condition, she felt a sense of control that helped to alleviate some of her fear.

Sarah also focused on self-care. She started practicing yoga and mindfulness, which helped her manage the anxiety that had been building inside. With Tom by her side, Sarah began to slowly rebuild her hope. They spent time together, cherishing the small victories, such as hearing the baby's heartbeat during a check-up.

The months passed, and although Sarah's pregnancy was still challenging, she began to regain a sense of optimism. She learned to be kind to herself, accepting that it was okay to feel sad, but also allowing space for hope. She communicated openly with Tom, and together they found strength in each other and their growing support network.

By the time Sarah reached the 6-month mark, her pregnancy was stable, and the complications had eased. Although the emotional scars of the experience would linger for some time, Sarah had learned the value of patience, hope, and self-compassion during a time of deep grief. She had come to understand that grief is a natural response to the unexpected and uncertain, and she emerged stronger, knowing that she could face whatever came next.

In this chapter, we will explore **tips** for coping with grief from pregnancy complications, with the understanding that the grief may last until the situation improves. These tips are designed to guide you through this difficult time and offer a path toward emotional healing.

Tips for Coping with Grief from Pregnancy Complications

1. Acknowledge and Accept Your Emotions

Pregnancy complications can stir up a variety of emotions, such as fear, sadness, guilt, or even anger. These emotions are completely normal. Allow yourself to feel without judgment. It's okay to grieve and mourn the uncertainty or loss of your plans for a healthy pregnancy.

Tip: Don't suppress your feelings. Give yourself permission to feel and express your emotions in healthy ways, whether it's through crying, journaling, or talking to someone you trust.

2. Find a Support System

Going through pregnancy complications can be isolating, but you don't have to face it alone. Reach out to your partner, friends, family, or support groups. Having a network of people who can offer emotional and practical support will help you cope with the emotional strain.

Tip: Don't hesitate to ask for help. Sometimes, just having someone to listen can ease your pain.

3. Educate Yourself About the Complications

Uncertainty often fuels fear, and understanding your condition or the nature of your pregnancy complications can reduce some of the anxiety. Knowledge can empower you, provide clarity, and help you understand what is happening.

Tip: Speak with your healthcare provider about your concerns and do research to learn more about the situation. Understanding the medical aspects can help you feel more in control.

4. Focus on What You Can Control

When facing complications, much of the situation feels out of your hands. However, there are things you can control, such as your self-care, your mindset, and how you manage your stress. Focus on what you can do to support yourself physically and emotionally.

Tip: Engage in relaxation techniques, eat nourishing foods, and rest. Creating a sense of control over your physical well-being can help alleviate emotional distress.

5. Allow Yourself to Grieve

It's okay to mourn the pregnancy as you had imagined it. You may be grieving the excitement of a smooth, uneventful pregnancy or even the dreams you had about this particular pregnancy. It's important to give yourself time and space to grieve and not rush the process.

Tip: Grief doesn't have a timeline. Allow yourself to feel sadness, but know that healing will come, and it's okay to take as much time as you need.

6. Limit Stress and Anxiety

Stress and anxiety can worsen the emotional burden of pregnancy complications. Finding ways to reduce stress through mindfulness, breathing exercises, and gentle movement can have a calming effect on both your mind and body.

Tip: Practice deep breathing, meditation, or yoga to reduce anxiety. These activities can help you stay centred and alleviate tension in your body.

7. Seek Professional Support

Therapy or counselling can provide a safe space to explore your emotions. A mental health professional can help you process your grief, manage anxiety, and develop coping strategies.

Tip: Don't hesitate to reach out to a therapist if you're feeling overwhelmed. Therapy can provide valuable guidance during challenging times.

8. Communicate with Your Partner

If you have a partner, it's important to communicate openly and honestly about how you're feeling. Pregnancy complications can strain relationships, so it's vital to support each other, share your fears, and work through the sadness together.

Tip: Share your concerns and fears with your partner. Talking openly about your feelings can strengthen your relationship and help both of you process the experience.

9. Be Kind to Yourself

During times of emotional distress, it's easy to be hard on yourself. You might feel guilty for being sad or frustrated, especially when you know others may be going through similar struggles. Remember, there is no right or wrong way to feel.

Tip: Practice self-compassion. Be gentle with yourself as you navigate through the ups and downs of this journey. Understand that you are doing the best you can.

10. Stay Hopeful, But Be Realistic

While it's important to remain hopeful for a positive outcome, it's also essential to accept that pregnancy complications may require time to resolve. Be realistic about the process, but also hold onto hope that things can improve.

Tip: Focus on small moments of hope and healing. Even in difficult times, positive change can happen, and each small improvement can serve as a reminder of your resilience.

Coping with grief from pregnancy complications is not an easy path, but with time, self-compassion, and support, you can manage your emotions and find hope for the future. Grief is a part of the process, but it doesn't define your journey. By focusing on healing, being kind to yourself, and allowing yourself the space to feel, you can navigate this challenging time with resilience and strength.

THE COPING CODE: COPING WITH GRIEF FROM BUSINESS READJUSTMENT

Maximum Period of Sadness: 5 Months

"The greatest glory in living lies not in never falling, but in rising every time we fall."

– Nelson Mandela

Facing a business readjustment, whether it's due to market changes, restructuring, or financial challenges, can be an emotional rollercoaster. For many entrepreneurs and business owners, their ventures are more than just a source of income—they are a passion, a personal achievement, and often a significant part of their identity. When business operations shift, the grief associated with this change can be profound. It may involve the loss of employees, clients, or the restructuring of a once-thriving company.

While the sadness that accompanies a business readjustment is real and valid, it's also temporary. The key is to recognize that the grief, while powerful, doesn't have to be permanent. It may take time to recover, but with the right mindset and steps, you can work through it and emerge stronger, more adaptable, and ready to navigate the new landscape. It's important to understand that the maximum period of sadness from a business readjustment is generally about six months. This period is not a fixed rule, but rather a guide that allows time for the initial emotional toll to ease and for the transition to move forward.

Lena had spent the last five years building her small but successful boutique marketing agency. She had hired a team she trusted, established loyal client relationships, and watched her business grow steadily. However, the landscape changed when the economy took a downturn, and many of her clients began cutting back on marketing expenses.

After months of trying to adapt, Lena was forced to make difficult decisions—laying off employees, reducing overhead, and reevaluating her services. It was a painful readjustment that left Lena feeling deeply sad. The agency had been her passion, and seeing it struggle was heartbreaking. She felt as though she had failed, as though all her hard work had led to nothing.

For the first time in years, Lena allowed herself to grieve. She took a week off from the business, stepping back from the overwhelming decisions to process her emotions. She cried, talked to her husband, and reached out to a few close friends who were also business owners. Their encouragement and advice reminded her that setbacks are a natural part of the journey.

Lena also focused on maintaining her health, making sure she ate well and took time for long walks to clear her head. One afternoon, as she walked along the beach, she had an epiphany—this setback was not the end, but a chance to reevaluate her business model. She began to shift her mindset from feeling defeated to feeling determined to reimagine the business.

Over the next few months, Lena worked on restructuring her services, focusing on niche areas where demand was still strong. She streamlined her team and brought in new digital tools to increase efficiency. With each small success—whether it was securing a new client or completing a successful rebranding—Lena began to feel more hopeful and empowered.

Six months after the business readjustment began, Lena was in a much better place. While the sadness and grief hadn't completely vanished, she had learned to view the experience as an opportunity for growth and reinvention. The business was no longer the same, but it was thriving in new ways. Lena realized that the grief of loss had transformed into the resilience needed to rise again.

In this chapter, we will explore **tips** to help cope with the grief caused by business readjustment, enabling you to rebuild, regroup, and rise again after setbacks.

Tips for Coping with Grief from Business Readjustment
1. Acknowledge the Grief

The first step in overcoming grief is to acknowledge it. Recognize that it's normal to feel sadness, frustration, and even anger when your business faces a setback. These emotions don't make you weak—they are a natural response to loss and change.

Tip: Permit yourself to feel the sadness. It's important to process these emotions instead of pushing them down.

2. Allow Yourself Time to Process

After a business readjustment, you may feel the weight of the changes and decisions that led to it. Give yourself time to grieve without rushing the process. Time is essential for healing, and your emotional recovery can only happen once you've had the space to reflect.

Tip: Take a few days off if needed to clear your mind. Use this time to assess your situation, think through your options, and let your feelings settle.

3. Focus on the Bigger Picture

Sometimes, focusing on the bigger picture can help you put things in perspective. While it's easy to focus on what's been lost or changed, take a step back and look at the long-term potential. Business readjustments can often lead to new opportunities, improvements, and growth.

Tip: Shift your focus from the immediate sadness to the future. Ask yourself how this setback could lead to a new, better direction for your business.

4. Talk to Someone You Trust

Grief can feel isolating, especially when it's tied to something so personal as a business. Sharing your feelings with someone you trust—whether it's a friend, family member, or fellow business owner—can help you feel heard and supported.

Tip: Have an open conversation about your grief. Talking about the changes can help you feel validated and begin the healing process.

5. Take Care of Your Health

The stress and sadness associated with business challenges can take a toll on your physical and mental health. It's important to prioritize self-care during this period, ensuring you're taking steps to maintain your well-being.

Tip: Make time for physical activity, eat well, and get enough rest. Self-care is essential for emotional recovery and for maintaining the energy you need to move forward.

6. Reframe Your Mindset

Instead of viewing the business readjustment as a failure, try to reframe your perspective. Consider it a necessary pivot or adjustment that could lead to even greater success. Many successful entrepreneurs have faced setbacks, but their resilience and ability to adapt allowed them to thrive in the long term.

Tip: Ask yourself, "What can I learn from this?" Shifting your mindset from failure to opportunity can make all the difference in how you recover.

7. Focus on What You Can Control

In times of uncertainty, it's easy to feel overwhelmed by everything outside of your control. Instead of stressing over uncontrollable aspects of the business adjustment, focus on what you can influence, such as your attitude, actions, and decisions going forward.

Tip: Create an action plan that focuses on the aspects you can control. This will give you a sense of purpose and direction as you rebuild.

8. Embrace Change

Business readjustments often signal the need for change. Change can be difficult, but it can also be a source of growth. Look at this as an opportunity to innovate, learn new strategies, and improve your business operations. Embrace the potential for positive change, even if it feels uncomfortable at first.

Tip: View change as a chance to reimagine your business in a way that could bring better results. Consider what's working, what isn't, and how you can innovate moving forward.

9. Seek Professional Support

Sometimes, the grief surrounding business readjustment requires professional guidance. Business coaches, financial advisors, or therapists specializing in business challenges can offer valuable insights and help you develop a strategy for overcoming the emotional and logistical hurdles.

Tip: Reach out to a business coach or mentor who can provide you with practical advice and help you process the emotional aspects of the transition.

10. Celebrate Small Wins

As you move through the process of readjustment, it's important to celebrate the small victories along the way. These wins may include signing new clients, finding efficiencies in your operations, or simply maintaining a positive mindset despite the challenges.

Tip: Recognize and celebrate even the smallest progress. Each step forward is a success, and acknowledging these victories will keep you motivated.

Coping with grief from business readjustment takes time, patience, and a willingness to embrace change. By following the tips outlined in this chapter, you can begin to heal and rebuild your business with a fresh perspective. Remember, it's okay to grieve, but it's also important to focus on the future and trust that this challenging time can lead to new opportunities and growth.

THE COPING CODE: COPING WITH GRIEF FROM A CHANGE IN FINANCIAL STATE

Maximum Period of Sadness: 4 Months

> *"It's not the strongest of the species that survive, nor the most intelligent, but the one most responsive to change."*
> **– Charles Darwin**

A change in your financial state, whether through job loss, a financial setback, or an unexpected life event, can create feelings of deep sadness and insecurity. Your financial stability is often tied to your sense of security, identity, and future well-being. When this stability is threatened or taken away, it can be incredibly overwhelming. This grief can take many forms, from anxiety about the future to sadness about what's been lost.

However, just like any form of grief, the emotional turmoil following a change in financial state doesn't have to last forever. The maximum period of sadness for this type of grief is generally about six months, although this period may vary depending on your circumstances. During this time, you will likely experience a range of emotions, including shock, fear, anger, and disappointment. But through understanding, support, and practical steps, you can regain control of your emotions and rebuild a sense of security and confidence.

Rachel had always prided herself on being financially secure. She had a steady job in marketing, and her husband, James, had his own successful freelance photography business. They lived comfortably, saved diligently, and planned for the future. But all of that changed when Rachel was laid off from her job due to company-wide budget cuts.

At first, Rachel was in shock. How could she lose her job? Her security, her identity, seemed to have been pulled out from under her. She was angry at the situation, worried about her future, and devastated by the uncertainty. Her sadness was compounded by James' slow-growing struggle to find steady clients for his photography business, leaving their household income in jeopardy.

For the first few weeks, Rachel could hardly get out of bed. She felt overwhelmed and defeated, unsure of how to face the world outside. However, after some time, she decided to start facing the situation head-on. She started by going through her finances, making a budget, and identifying areas where she could cut back. While it wasn't easy, she found some comfort in knowing exactly where she stood.

Rachel also reached out to a financial advisor, who helped her create a plan to stabilize her finances. With the advisor's help, she was able to take steps toward reducing debt and starting a small emergency savings fund. It was a relief to have a tangible plan in place, and she felt a little more in control of her circumstances.

Over the next few months, Rachel's emotional grief began to ease. She took up yoga and meditation to reduce her stress, reconnected with old friends, and focused on developing new skills. As she expanded her network, she found freelance marketing opportunities that helped supplement the family's income. Slowly but surely, she began to regain confidence in herself and her ability to overcome challenges.

By the end of six months, Rachel had not only found new professional opportunities but also developed a more resilient mindset. While things weren't the same as before, she had learned to embrace the uncertainty and trust in her ability to adapt. With a renewed sense of purpose, Rachel and James were able to rebuild their financial foundation and move forward together.

This chapter will offer **important tips** for overcoming the grief caused by a change in your financial state, helping you not only cope with your emotions but also regain a sense of empowerment and hope for the future.

Tips for Coping with Grief from a Change in Financial State

1. Acknowledge the Emotional Impact

Financial changes often come with a deep emotional toll. It's important to recognize and accept the grief and stress you may be feeling. Whether it's fear, embarrassment, or sadness, allowing yourself to feel these emotions is the first step toward healing.

Tip: Be gentle with yourself. Recognizing your feelings without judgment can help you begin to process and move forward.

2. Take Small Steps Toward Financial Clarity

When faced with financial uncertainty, it can feel paralyzing. But the sooner you face the reality of your situation; the sooner you can take control. Start by reviewing your finances—make a list of income, expenses, and assets. This will help you gain clarity and create a plan moving forward.

Tip: Create a detailed budget and look for areas where you can cut back. Knowing where you stand financially is crucial to making informed decisions about the future.

3. Seek Professional Financial Guidance

If your financial situation is significantly impacted, seeking advice from a financial advisor or counsellor can provide much-needed perspective. They can help you navigate the best course of action, such as debt management, savings adjustments, and long-term planning.

Tip: Don't hesitate to seek professional guidance. A financial expert can provide strategies that you might not have considered on your own.

4. Focus on What You Can Control

Financial changes often create a sense of helplessness. It's crucial to focus on aspects of your situation that you can control. While you can't always control market forces or economic downturns, you can control your spending, saving habits, and even your career path.

Tip: Make a list of actions you can take to improve your situation. Taking small steps each day can help you feel more in control of your finances and your emotional well-being.

5. Reframe Your Mindset

While it may seem impossible in the moment, try to reframe the situation. A change in your financial state, though difficult, may present new opportunities. Many people have found success after overcoming financial struggles—by embracing a fresh perspective, you too can rise from the ashes of this challenge.

Tip: Instead of viewing your financial change as a permanent setback, see it as an opportunity for growth and reinvention. What new paths can you explore? How can you learn from this?

6. Talk to Someone You Trust

Sharing your worries and concerns with a trusted friend, family member, or therapist can help lighten the emotional load. Talking through your feelings can also provide you with new perspectives and advice that may help you feel more supported.

Tip: Reach out to someone who is a good listener. Even if they can't offer a solution, the act of expressing your emotions will help you feel validated and understood.

7. Embrace Your Support System

Financial difficulties affect not just you but your loved ones as well. While it's natural to want to protect your family from your stress, it's important to lean on them for support. Sharing your struggles with your partner, children, or close friends can deepen your relationships and help you feel less isolated.

Tip: Be open with your support system about your struggles. Let them know how they can help and offer them the chance to comfort you.

8. Stay Active and Engaged

When you're feeling overwhelmed by financial grief, it's easy to retreat into isolation. However, staying physically and mentally active can help lift your spirits and combat negative emotions. Exercise, engage in hobbies, and spend time with others to maintain a positive outlook.

Tip: Try to set aside time for activities that make you feel good. Whether it's taking a walk, reading, or volunteering, keeping yourself engaged will reduce stress and help you feel more in control.

9. Set Realistic Goals

After a change in your financial state, it's easy to feel overwhelmed by the sheer number of things that need to be fixed or accomplished. Break down your financial recovery into smaller, achievable goals. Each small success will build momentum and help you regain a sense of progress.

Tip: Set short-term goals that are attainable. For example, aim to reduce your expenses by a certain percentage or create a plan for increasing your income in the next few months.

10. Practice Patience and Self-Compassion

Recovering from a financial setback takes time. It's important to be patient with yourself as you navigate this challenging period. Self-compassion is key—don't beat yourself up for being in this situation, and remember that recovery is a gradual process.

Tip: Treat yourself with kindness. Understand that it may take time to heal emotionally and financially, but with effort and patience, you will emerge stronger.

Coping with grief from a change in your financial state can feel like an insurmountable challenge. However, by following these steps—acknowledging the emotional impact, seeking support, staying active, and setting realistic goals—you can heal and emerge from this difficult period even stronger than before. With time, patience, and perseverance, you'll find that your financial setback can become a stepping stone to a brighter, more resilient future.

THE COPING CODE: COPING WITH GRIEF FROM A MAJOR MORTGAGE

Maximum Period of Sadness: 4 Months

"The best way to predict your future is to create it."
— **Abraham Lincoln**

A major mortgage, whether due to taking on a large home loan or a drastic change in your financial circumstances, can create feelings of intense stress, fear, and sadness. The weight of an overwhelming mortgage can lead to sleepless nights, worries about future payments, and even doubts about your financial future. It's not just about the house; it's about the security and the life you've built around it. When things go wrong, it can feel like the foundation of your life is shaking beneath you.

However, the grief you feel as a result of a major mortgage doesn't have to last forever. While it may take time to adjust, the maximum period of sadness is typically about six months. Within that time, you can find ways to cope with your emotions, reevaluate your options, and regain control of your finances. The process is one of recovery, empowerment, and resilience, and in this chapter, you'll find practical tips to guide you through this challenging period.

Sarah and Mark had always dreamed of owning a home. After years of renting, they finally purchased their dream house. It was spacious, well-located, and full of potential. They were proud of what they had achieved and excited to start their new life.

But just a few months after moving in, Mark's business began to struggle. A series of bad contracts and lost clients put a significant dent in their income. The couple found themselves living pay check to pay check, barely scraping by to make their hefty mortgage payments.

The first few weeks were filled with panic. Sarah couldn't sleep, constantly worrying about how they'd make the next payment. They tried cutting back on unnecessary expenses, but it didn't seem to make enough of a difference. Their mortgage loomed over them like a heavy weight, and the stress began to take a toll on their relationship. Mark, feeling embarrassed, withdrew emotionally, and Sarah grew resentful.

One night, overwhelmed by the situation, Sarah sat down and reviewed their finances. She made a list of their income, expenses, debts, and savings. The exercise didn't immediately solve their problems, but it provided clarity. Sarah realized that they had a bit of savings they could tap into and that they weren't alone—many homeowners faced similar struggles.

The next step was to reach out to their lender. Mark and Sarah nervously called the bank, but to their surprise, the bank offered them a temporary forbearance. This relief gave them some breathing room, allowing them to catch up on bills and focus on finding a solution. They also contacted a financial advisor, who helped them create a long-term plan to refinance their mortgage and manage their debt more effectively.

With a solid financial strategy in place, Sarah and Mark started feeling more in control. Over the next few months, they cut back on non-essential spending, sought additional work, and adjusted their lifestyle to live more sustainably. Although they were still adjusting, their financial outlook began to improve, and the constant worry started to ease.

Six months later, while they were still working on rebuilding their finances, Sarah and Mark had regained a sense of stability. They learned valuable lessons about budgeting, communication, and the importance of seeking help when needed. More importantly, they felt closer to one another, having worked together to overcome the hardship.

Tips for Coping with Grief from a Major Mortgage

1. Acknowledge Your Emotions

It's essential to allow yourself to feel the emotions that come with the stress of a major mortgage. Whether it's anxiety, fear, frustration, or sadness, recognizing and accepting your emotions is the first step in moving forward.

Tip: Permit yourself to feel upset. It's normal to grieve the situation before taking steps toward resolution.

2. Take a Deep Breath and Assess the Situation

Facing a significant mortgage payment can feel overwhelming, but it's important to take a step back and assess your financial situation calmly. Review your income, expenses, and mortgage terms. Having a clear understanding of where you stand can help you make informed decisions moving forward.

Tip: Create a financial inventory. This means knowing your monthly expenses, debts, and any assets you can leverage.

3. Reach Out to Your Lender

If you're struggling with payments or your mortgage is feeling unmanageable, don't shy away from speaking with your lender. Many lenders have programs in place for homeowners in financial distress. They may be able to offer loan modifications, forbearance, or other forms of assistance.

Tip: Be proactive. Lenders often appreciate early communication and may be more willing to work with you if you reach out before things become dire.

4. Set a Realistic Budget

Review your spending and create a strict budget to help you manage your finances more effectively. Identify areas where you can cut back and allocate those savings toward your mortgage or other essential expenses.

Tip: Prioritize your mortgage payment while trimming non-essential expenses. A strict budget will give you more breathing room financially.

5. Consider Refinancing

If interest rates have dropped or your financial situation has improved, refinancing your mortgage may lower your monthly payments or allow you to consolidate debt. This can help ease the financial burden and reduce your stress.

Tip: Research refinancing options. Consulting with a financial advisor can help you determine whether this is the right choice for you.

6. Seek Professional Financial Advice

Consulting with a financial advisor can provide you with strategies to manage your mortgage and overall financial situation. A professional can offer guidance on budgeting, debt management, and long-term financial planning.

Tip: Work with a professional who specializes in debt management and mortgage issues. They can offer specific advice based on your unique situation.

7. Focus on What You Can Control

While you can't control all aspects of your financial situation, focusing on what you *can* control will help you feel more empowered. Whether it's reducing your spending, negotiating with creditors, or finding additional sources of income, taking small actions can provide you with a sense of progress.

Tip: Identify the things within your control, such as limiting impulse spending or seeking freelance work to supplement your income.

8. Find Emotional Support

Dealing with a major mortgage is not only a financial burden but an emotional one as well. It's important to have a support system that can provide encouragement and perspective during this difficult time. Talking to a friend, family member, or therapist can help relieve emotional stress.

Tip: Open up to someone you trust. Sometimes, simply talking about the situation can alleviate the emotional weight.

9. Take Time to Recharge

The stress of a major mortgage can take a toll on your physical and mental well-being. It's important to take time for self-care. Whether it's getting regular exercise, practicing relaxation techniques, or simply taking a day off to unwind, make sure you're taking care of yourself.

Tip: Prioritize self-care. Even small activities like walking or taking a hot bath can help reduce stress and improve your outlook.

10. Create a Long-Term Plan for Stability

Though the current situation may feel daunting, creating a long-term financial plan can provide you with a sense of direction and hope. Set both short-term and long-term goals for your financial future, and take steps toward achieving them.

Tip: Break down your long-term goals into smaller, actionable steps. Having a plan can help you regain a sense of control over your financial future.

Dealing with grief from a major mortgage can be one of the most stressful and emotional experiences of your life. However, by acknowledging your emotions, reaching out for help, and taking proactive steps to address the situation, you can reduce the sadness and move forward with confidence. With time and patience, you'll find that you are stronger and more resilient than you ever thought possible.

THE COPING CODE: COPING WITH GRIEF FROM CHANGE IN RESPONSIBILITIES AT WORK

Maximum Period of Sadness: 4 Months

"The measure of who we are is what we do with what we have."

– Vince Lombardi

A sudden change in responsibilities at work can bring about feelings of sadness, stress, and confusion. Whether it's being promoted to a new leadership role, taking on more tasks than you're prepared for, or even being reassigned to a role you didn't expect or desire, the grief from such changes can be intense. We all define ourselves by our work to some degree, and when that work changes unexpectedly, it can feel as if part of our identity is in jeopardy.

Such transitions often feel like a loss, whether it's the loss of autonomy, purpose, or passion. However, this grief doesn't have to last forever. In fact, with the right mindset and strategies, you can navigate this period of sadness and come out of it with greater clarity and resilience. The maximum period of sadness for this kind of grief is often about six months, giving you time to adjust, reflect, and find your path forward.

Maya had been working in sales at her company for over eight years. She loved her job—meeting clients, creating presentations, and closing deals. Over time, she had built a solid reputation for herself and developed a sense of pride in her accomplishments. Her role had become a part of her identity, and she was content with the trajectory her career was on.

But everything changed one fateful Tuesday morning when Maya's manager informed her that her role would be restructured as part of a broader company initiative. Instead of focusing on client acquisition, Maya would now be responsible for training and mentoring new sales associates. While it was still within the sales department, the change felt like a step backward for Maya. She no longer felt the thrill of closing deals and the recognition that came with it. Her identity, wrapped up in her sales accomplishments, suddenly felt disconnected from her new responsibilities.

At first, Maya resisted the change. She was disappointed, angry, and even felt a bit betrayed by the company she had worked so hard for. She spent the next few days in a fog, questioning her worth and feeling disconnected from her work. The sadness she felt seemed all-consuming, and she couldn't shake the feeling that she had lost her place within the company.

The Coping Code: Coping With Grief From Change in Responsibilities At Work

One evening, after a particularly tough day, Maya decided to reflect on the situation. She recognized that her sadness stemmed not only from the loss of the excitement she once felt but also from her fear of being stuck in a role she wasn't passionate about. But as she processed these feelings, she began to see things differently. She realized that the company had placed its trust in her to help others succeed, and that was an honour. While the new role didn't bring the same thrill, it offered the opportunity to mentor others and shape the future of the sales team. Maya also realized that the change gave her a chance to develop new leadership skills and expand her professional growth in areas she hadn't previously considered.

Determined to make the best of the situation, Maya took her manager up on an offer for leadership training. She also sought advice from a colleague who had made a similar transition in the past. Slowly, Maya began to adapt to her new responsibilities, setting small goals for herself and celebrating each success along the way.

Six months later, Maya had not only grown comfortable in her new role but had also discovered a passion for mentoring that she hadn't known existed. She had learned new skills, built deeper relationships with her colleagues, and felt more connected to her company than ever before. What had initially felt like a loss had turned into an opportunity for growth, and Maya realized that sometimes the most challenging changes lead to the most rewarding transformations.

Tips for Coping with Grief from a Change in Responsibilities at Work

1. Allow Yourself to Grieve

It's essential to acknowledge the emotional impact of the change in your work responsibilities. Denying or suppressing your feelings may only prolong your grief. Take the time to process the sadness and frustrations you're experiencing.

Tip: Permit yourself to feel disappointed and upset, but make a commitment to move forward when the time is right.

2. Reflect on the Change

Understanding the reasons behind the change can help you process it more effectively. Ask yourself what has shifted and why. Was it part of a company-wide decision, or is it something that aligns with your personal goals?

Tip: Write about your feelings in a journal to gain insight into how the change impacts you, both personally and professionally.

3. See It as an Opportunity

While the change might feel negative initially, it may also bring new opportunities. A new role might help you build skills you hadn't developed before. Rather than focusing on the loss, try to identify what you can gain from the shift.

Tip: Reframe your perspective and ask yourself what new skills or experiences you could acquire in your new role.

4. Communicate with Your Manager

Understanding why the change was made can help you regain a sense of control. Have a conversation with your supervisor to clarify expectations and discuss how you can adapt to the new responsibilities.

Tip: Use the conversation to ask for additional training or support if you feel unprepared or uncertain about your new tasks.

5. Set Clear New Goals

If your role has changed, take the time to reassess your career goals. Consider what you hope to achieve in this new position and set both short-term and long-term goals. This will help you stay focused and provide you with a sense of direction.

Tip: Write down your new goals and create an action plan to achieve them. Break them down into smaller, manageable tasks to avoid feeling overwhelmed.

6. Seek Support from Colleagues and Mentors

Sometimes the best way to cope with a change is to talk about it. Reaching out to colleagues or mentors who have experienced similar transitions can provide you with valuable advice and emotional support.

Tip: Join a professional group or find a mentor who can help guide you through this period of change.

7. Take Time to Reflect on Your Career Path

A shift in responsibilities can be a great opportunity for personal reflection. Ask yourself if the new role aligns with your long-term career aspirations. This could be the perfect time to reassess your overall career direction and adjust your goals.

Tip: Take some time off to think about whether you want to pursue this new direction or if this change has opened up the possibility for exploring other career paths.

8. Build a Support System

Whether it's friends, family, or a professional network, having a support system can help you navigate the emotional impact of this change. Talking to others who care about you can alleviate feelings of isolation and give you strength during this time.

Tip: Let your loved ones know what you're going through. Having emotional support can make the transition feel less daunting.

9. Take Care of Your Physical and Mental Health

Stress and anxiety from work changes can take a toll on your physical and mental well-being. Make sure to take care of yourself by eating well, getting regular exercise, and practicing relaxation techniques like deep breathing or meditation.

Tip: Schedule time for physical activity and mindfulness practices to manage stress and stay focused.

10. Be Patient with Yourself

Adjusting to new responsibilities can take time, and it's important to be patient with yourself during this period. Give yourself grace and understand that it's normal to experience some frustration and sadness during the adjustment process.

Tip: Set realistic expectations for yourself. It's okay if you don't immediately feel comfortable in your new role. Progress takes time.

A change in responsibilities at work can initially bring about grief, but with the right approach, this grief can be short-lived. By acknowledging your emotions, reflecting on the situation, and taking proactive steps to adjust, you can transform this period of sadness into an opportunity for personal and professional growth.

THE COPING CODE: COPING WITH GRIEF FROM A CHILD LEAVING HOME

Maximum Period of Sadness: 4 Months

"The hardest part of loving someone is knowing when to let go."

– **Anonymous**

The moment your child leaves home, whether it's for college, a job, or moving out to start a new life, it's an emotional shift that can be deeply unsettling. You've watched them grow, protected them, and been an integral part of their daily lives. Suddenly, you may find yourself feeling lost, grieving the physical absence, and adjusting to a new phase in your relationship.

The sadness that comes with this life transition is normal and valid. It represents the end of one chapter and the beginning of another. You're not just mourning the change in daily routines; you're grieving the shift in your identity as a parent. The good news is that the pain is temporary. Most parents experience the deepest sadness within the first three months after their child leaves home. Over time, the grief lessens, and you'll find new ways to connect with your child and rediscover yourself in this new stage of life.

Claire and David had always known this day would come. Their youngest child, Emma, had just been accepted to her dream university in another state. For years, they had talked about this moment, envisioning it as a time for Emma to take on new challenges and for them to finally have some "empty nest" freedom. But now that the moment was real, Claire felt an overwhelming wave of sadness that she hadn't anticipated.

It wasn't that Claire wasn't proud of Emma. She was. Emma had worked hard to get into a prestigious university, and Claire knew this was the next step toward the future she had dreamed of for her daughter. But as Claire watched Emma pack up her belongings, ready to leave for the semester, a deep ache settled in her chest. The house felt suddenly too quiet. There would be no more late-night chats, no more driving Emma to school events, and no more hearing her laugh from the other room.

The first week after Emma left, Claire found herself wandering through the house, lost in memories of her daughter's childhood. The silence was deafening. She would often sit in Emma's room, hugging the pillow that still smelled like her shampoo, fighting back tears.

David noticed the sadness in Claire but didn't know how to help. He gently suggested they start planning their own activities—maybe take a weekend trip or spend more time with friends—but

Claire wasn't ready for that. She wanted to hold on to her role as a mother, a caretaker.

But after a few weeks, Claire started taking small steps to adjust. She and David started revisiting old hobbies they had neglected over the years, like gardening and hiking. Claire also used the time to reconnect with her own interests, spending hours reading books she had put off and taking an art class she had always wanted to try. As time passed, she found joy in rediscovering herself outside of being "Mom."

After three months, Claire was still sad but no longer overwhelmed by grief. She had found new rhythms in her life and had a stronger connection with David. Emma, too, was thriving in her new environment, calling regularly to share her experiences. Claire realized that the sadness had not gone away entirely, but it had shifted into a more manageable feeling of longing for her daughter's presence.

One weekend, Emma returned home for a visit. Claire was surprised by how much they both enjoyed the time together, but she also realized that they had both changed. Their relationship had evolved, and Claire now saw how independent and capable Emma had become. Though Claire still missed the chaos of family life, she now embraced this new phase, knowing that her child would always be part of her heart, no matter where life took her.

Tips for Coping with Grief from a Child Leaving Home

1. Allow Yourself to Feel

Don't suppress your emotions or feel guilty about feeling sad. It's okay to cry, be upset, and acknowledge the void that your child's absence creates. Grief is a natural response to change.

Tip: Permit yourself to feel the sadness fully without judgment. Your emotions are valid.

2. Reframe the Change as Growth

Instead of focusing on what you've lost, consider what this change means for your child's growth and independence. Celebrate the fact that they are taking the next step in their journey.

Tip: Reflect on how proud you are of your child for embarking on this next adventure. Their independence is a sign of your success as a parent.

3. Maintain Communication

Stay in touch with your child, but let them have the space they need to settle into their new life. Regular check-ins through calls, texts, or video chats can help maintain the bond without feeling like you're smothering them.

Tip: Schedule regular but non-intrusive communication times. Let them initiate contact when they're ready, but keep your connection strong.

4. Create New Routines

The space left behind can create a sense of loss. To cope with the emptiness, try filling that void with new routines. You could take up a hobby, focus more on your career, or dedicate time to self-care activities you didn't have time for before.

Tip: Try to fill your home with positive activities that bring you joy or peace. Create a new schedule that allows you to focus on yourself.

5. Rediscover Your Own Identity

As a parent, it's easy to become defined by your child's needs and activities. Now that your child is away, it's a good time to reconnect with yourself. Focus on rediscovering hobbies, passions, or goals that may have been put on hold.

Tip: Use this time to re-explore your interests and goals. Whether it's taking a cooking class, going back to school, or traveling, make space for things that matter to you.

6. Celebrate Their Independence

Understand that this transition is also a victory for your child. They are embarking on a new chapter of their life, and their leaving signifies a step forward in their personal development.

Tip: Celebrate your child's accomplishments and the fact that you've helped them reach this milestone. Consider giving them a small gift or sending a care package to show your continued support.

7. Be Open to New Experiences Together

While your child's physical presence may be missed, you can still create new types of experiences with them. Instead of just focusing on the absence, plan activities for when they visit or when you visit them.

Tip: Plan future visits or activities, like trips or weekend getaways, to make the time you do spend together meaningful.

8. Embrace the Quiet

Initially, the silence might feel overwhelming, but with time, the quiet will become something to appreciate. You can now enjoy moments of peace and tranquillity, something that might have been hard to come by when the house was full.

Tip: Practice mindfulness in the quiet moments. Use this time to reflect, relax, and recharge.

9. Lean on Your Support System

Talk to friends and family members who have gone through the same experience. Sharing your feelings with others who understand can provide comfort, and it can also remind you that you're not alone in this.

Tip: Seek out support groups or friends who can relate. It's comforting to know that others have walked this path and found ways to cope.

10. Focus on Your Relationship with Your Partner

If you have a partner, this is an excellent time to reconnect and strengthen your bond. With your child no longer at home, you can focus on spending quality time with your partner and rediscover your relationship outside of your roles as parents.

Tip: Schedule regular date nights or activities with your partner. This can reignite the connection and help ease the transition.

The grief of a child leaving home is profound, but it is temporary. With time, self-reflection, and new experiences, you'll discover that the sadness evolves into a more manageable, bittersweet feeling. Allow yourself to grieve, but also celebrate the growth of both your child and yourself. The transition is difficult, but it opens the door to new beginnings and deeper connections in both your relationship with your child and yourself.

THE COPING CODE: COPING WITH GRIEF DUE TO TROUBLE WITH IN-LAWS

Maximum Period of Sadness: 4 Months

"Family is not an important thing. It's everything."
— **Michael J. Fox**

When you're experiencing conflict with your in-laws, it can feel like you're caught in a difficult, emotional tug-of-war. You want to support your partner and maintain family harmony, but the friction with your in-laws can lead to frustration, hurt feelings, and a sense of isolation. Whether the issues stem from misunderstandings, clashing personalities, or longstanding family dynamics, the strain it places on your relationship can feel overwhelming.

It's essential to acknowledge that the grief and sadness that arise from in-law issues are valid. These conflicts can create feelings of being torn between loyalty to your spouse and wanting peace in the family. However, the sadness is temporary, and with time, communication, and patience, you can navigate through the difficulties and emerge stronger. The key to healing from this type of grief is recognizing the situation for what it is and choosing to set boundaries, practice empathy, and make space for emotional growth.

Jane and John had always had a close-knit relationship, but when they got married, Jane quickly found herself at odds with John's family. His parents had high expectations for their son, and while John was supportive of Jane, his family constantly questioned her choices, opinions, and values. Over time, Jane found herself feeling increasingly isolated from her in-laws, and the tension began to affect her relationship with John.

It wasn't just small disagreements – the criticisms from his parents were often pointed and hurtful. At family gatherings, Jane would feel like an outsider, as if she was being scrutinized every moment. She tried to keep the peace for the sake of her marriage, but the situation was draining. The more Jane tried to please them, the more they seemed to distance themselves, which left her feeling rejected and powerless.

For several months, Jane bottled up her emotions, thinking it was just a phase. But when the tension reached a breaking point during a holiday dinner, Jane finally broke down in front of John. She admitted that she felt unsupported and emotionally exhausted, and that the situation with his family was starting to negatively impact her mental health.

John was shocked but also grateful that Jane had opened up. He didn't realize the extent of the impact the conflict was having on her. He reassured her that he was on her side and promised to help mediate the relationship with his parents. Together, they set boundaries with his family, explaining that while Jane wanted to have a healthy relationship with them, she could no longer tolerate the constant criticisms.

In the following months, Jane focused on healing. She and John attended couples therapy, where they learned how to better communicate with one another. Jane also took time for herself, going on walks and spending time with friends to clear her mind. Over time, the grief of dealing with her in-laws' disapproval lessened. She and John found a new equilibrium, with Jane feeling more supported and less isolated.

While the relationship with John's parents never became perfect, Jane learned how to establish healthy boundaries. With time, the sadness she initially felt shifted into a place of acceptance. She understood that she could love her partner without needing to be loved by everyone in his family.

Tips for Coping with Grief Due to Trouble with In-Laws

1. Acknowledge Your Feelings

It's important to allow yourself to feel upset, frustrated, or even hurt. Dealing with family conflict, especially with in-laws, can be emotionally exhausting. Don't suppress your feelings, as doing so can lead to resentment over time.

Tip: Permit yourself to feel what you're feeling. Conflicting emotions are natural in this situation, and acknowledging them will help you process them.

2. Communicate Openly with Your Partner

Your partner is likely the key person who can help mediate the situation. Open, honest, and respectful communication is essential in these moments. Express your feelings without placing blame, and make sure to listen to their perspective as well.

Tip: Approach the conversation with empathy and a willingness to understand your partner's feelings. Work together to find a solution that supports both of your needs.

3. Set Healthy Boundaries

Establish boundaries with your in-laws to protect your mental health and relationship. It's okay to limit the time you spend with them or to set clear guidelines for respectful interactions. Your emotional well-being should always be a priority.

Tip: Define what is acceptable behaviour and what is not, and communicate those boundaries calmly. You don't have to tolerate negative behaviour from anyone, including in-laws.

4. Seek Compromise, Not Perfection

While it may not be possible to resolve every issue, finding a middle ground can help. Try to focus on areas where compromise is possible and let go of the idea that everything must be perfect. Not all conflicts can be fully resolved, but you can work toward minimizing the emotional damage.

Tip: Be realistic about what can be changed and what needs to be accepted. It's more about finding peace than achieving perfection.

5. Don't Let the Conflict Define Your Relationship

It's important to remember that the conflict with in-laws is just one part of your relationship with your partner. Don't let it overshadow the love, support, and connection you share. Focus on strengthening your bond and keep in mind that the relationship with your in-laws is separate from your marriage.

Tip: Reinforce the positives in your relationship with your partner. Let your shared love be stronger than external conflicts.

6. Practice Empathy

Try to understand where your in-laws are coming from. Often, conflict arises from a lack of understanding, differing expectations, or cultural differences. Stepping into their shoes can help you respond with patience and kindness, which can de-escalate the tension.

Tip: Practice active listening when speaking to your in-laws and show empathy. Sometimes, people just want to feel heard.

7. Don't Engage in Drama

Avoid getting caught in the drama or feeding into negativity. If your in-laws are being critical or toxic, it's important not to engage in those behaviours yourself. Responding with anger or defensiveness can only escalate the situation.

Tip: Keep your interactions calm and polite, even when the other party may be behaving poorly. Responding with grace helps maintain your dignity and emotional balance.

8. Find Support Elsewhere

Talking to trusted friends or a therapist can provide a fresh perspective on the situation and help you process your emotions in a healthy way. It's important to have a support system outside of the conflict so you don't feel isolated.

Tip: Lean on friends or a therapist to help you navigate the emotional turmoil. Sometimes an outside perspective can help you see things more clearly.

9. Take Care of Yourself

Grief caused by conflict with in-laws can take a toll on your mental and physical health. Make sure to prioritize self-care by engaging in activities that make you feel grounded, like exercise, meditation, journaling, or taking a walk in nature.

Tip: Make self-care a non-negotiable part of your routine. Taking care of your body and mind will help you stay resilient through this difficult time.

10. Give It Time

As with all forms of grief, time is a critical factor in healing. The intensity of the sadness you feel from the conflict with your in-laws will fade, but it may take a few months for you to feel emotionally balanced again. Be patient with yourself and the situation.

Tip: Allow yourself time to heal. Recognize that healing from grief doesn't happen overnight, but with time, you will feel better.

The grief from trouble with in-laws can be emotionally intense and challenging, but it is temporary. By allowing yourself to feel your emotions, communicating openly with your partner, setting boundaries, and practicing patience, you can overcome the sadness. Remember, the strength of your relationship with your spouse can withstand external pressures, and with time, you will find peace and understanding.

THE COPING CODE: COPING WITH GRIEF DUE TO A FAMILY MEMBER'S SUICIDE ATTEMPT

Maximum Period of Sadness: 3 Months

"Out of the mountain of despair, a stone of hope."
— **Martin Luther King Jr.**

When a family member attempts suicide, it can feel like the earth beneath you has shifted. It's a devastating, heart-wrenching experience that leaves you filled with confusion, guilt, and deep sadness. The shock of the event, along with the overwhelming emotions that follow, can make it difficult to understand how to navigate through this painful journey. But, like all grief, this sadness is temporary, and while it can take time, healing is possible.

In such moments, the grief experienced isn't just about the attempt itself, but about the fear and uncertainty that come with it. You may question what went wrong, whether you missed signs, or if there's something more you could have done. These thoughts are natural, but it's important to know that you're not alone in your sadness. Many people go through similar feelings, and with time, empathy, self-care, and professional support, you can move through this grief and find healing.

Julia had always been close to her younger brother, Ben. They shared everything, from childhood secrets to their dreams for the future. But everything changed one summer afternoon when Julia received a phone call no one ever expected: Ben had attempted suicide.

The news hit Julia like a freight train. She was flooded with confusion, disbelief, and guilt. How had she missed the signs? Why hadn't she been able to prevent this? Her mind raced with questions, each one more painful than the last. For days, she found it hard to focus, and everything felt out of place. Her heart ached for her brother, but at the same time, she couldn't shake the sadness that overwhelmed her.

Julia felt like she was drowning in emotions, unable to talk to anyone about what she was going through. She withdrew from her friends and avoided family gatherings. She didn't know how to process the intensity of the sadness or how to support Ben while also taking care of herself.

After a week of spiralling, Julia reached out to her close friend, Mia. Mia listened patiently, letting Julia express everything she had been bottling up. "It's okay to feel this way, Julia," Mia said softly. "You're not alone in this. And you don't have to carry the weight of the world on your shoulders."

Encouraged by her friend's words, Julia sought professional help. A therapist helped her understand the complexities of her grief and reminded her that it was okay to feel overwhelmed. The grief she was experiencing was not only about Ben's attempt but also the emotional toll of watching a loved one suffer.

Through therapy, Julia learned to set boundaries with herself and with others. She realized that it was okay to take time for self-care, and that she could still be there for Ben without sacrificing her own emotional well-being. Slowly, she began to heal, taking things one step at a time.

As the weeks passed, Julia also found the strength to communicate more openly with Ben. She encouraged him to share his feelings, offering him unconditional love and support. Though the road to recovery was long, Julia held onto the hope that things would improve.

Six months later, while the sadness wasn't completely gone, Julia could feel herself slowly letting go of the weight she had carried. She had learned to live with the grief, but she had also learned how to find hope again, both for herself and for Ben.

Tips for Coping with Grief Due to a Family Member's Suicide Attempt

1. Acknowledge Your Feelings

The emotions you're experiencing – shock, confusion, guilt, anger, and sadness – are valid. It's important to acknowledge what you feel, without suppressing your emotions. Denying your grief only prolongs the pain.

Tip: Permit yourself to experience the full range of emotions. It's okay to feel upset, sad, or even angry. These feelings will pass when you allow yourself to grieve.

2. Seek Professional Help

Grieving from a suicide attempt can be complex, and it's essential to get the right support. Talking to a therapist or counsellor can provide a safe space to process the grief, and help you understand how to cope with the emotional aftermath.

Tip: Don't hesitate to reach out to a professional who can guide you through your emotions and offer practical coping strategies.

3. Take Care of Your Mental Health

While it's natural to be concerned about your family member's well-being, you must also prioritize your own mental health. Practicing self-care – whether through meditation, exercise, or spending time with loved ones – will help keep you grounded and emotionally strong.

Tip: Regularly engage in activities that help you relax and recharge, such as yoga, journaling, or listening to calming music.

4. Open Up to Supportive People

Talking to others who understand and support you can be incredibly healing. Sharing your grief with trusted friends, family members, or a support group can lighten the emotional burden and remind you that you're not alone in this journey.

Tip: Seek out a trusted person you can confide in – whether that's a friend, partner, or counsellor. Expressing your emotions aloud can often help relieve the heaviness you carry inside.

5. Understand the Complexity of Suicide Attempts

It's important to recognize that suicide attempts are not the result of one single factor. Many things – including mental health struggles, personal trauma, or even biochemical imbalances – can contribute to such decisions. Understanding that your family member's pain led them to make this choice can help you navigate the grief without internalizing blame.

Tip: Accept that you cannot control or fix the circumstances that led to this moment. The important thing is to focus on supporting both yourself and your family member as they recover.

6. Establish Boundaries

While it's important to support your family member, it's equally crucial to set boundaries to protect your emotional well-being. If you're overwhelmed, it's okay to ask for help from other family members, professionals, or friends.

Tip: If necessary, set limits on how much you can emotionally invest at any given time. Allow yourself breaks to avoid burnout.

7. Give Yourself Time to Heal

Grief takes time. While it may feel urgent to "fix" the situation or move past the sadness, remember that it's okay to take the time you need to heal. Everyone's timeline for healing is different, and that's okay.

Tip: Allow yourself to grieve without rushing through it. Healing is a process, and with time, your emotions will become more manageable.

8. Encourage Open Communication

Once your family member is ready, it's important to create an open, non-judgmental space for them to express their thoughts and feelings. However, it's equally important for you to communicate your feelings with them, letting them know how deeply their attempt impacted you and the family.

Tip: Practice compassionate communication. Express your emotions, but also listen with empathy when your family member is ready to share their experience.

9. Focus on Hope and Healing

While it's normal to feel overwhelmed by sadness, it's crucial to keep hope at the centre of your focus. Recovery is possible, both for your family member and you. Over time, things will improve, and with appropriate treatment, emotional recovery is achievable.

Tip: Use affirmations or positive reminders to remind yourself that healing is possible for both you and your family member. Hold onto the hope that things will get better with time.

10. Find a Way to Honor Your Emotions

Grieving from a family member's suicide attempt isn't linear, and it's essential to express your grief in ways that feel healing to you. Whether through creative outlets like writing, art, or physical activity, finding a way to honour your emotions can help ease your pain.

Tip: Find an outlet – such as a journal, a walk in nature, or a hobby you love – to channel your grief in a healthy way.

Dealing with the aftermath of a family member's suicide attempt is one of the most painful forms of grief. It's important to permit yourself to grieve, seek professional support, and prioritize your mental health. Healing doesn't happen overnight, but with time, communication, and self-care, you can move through this difficult period and come out stronger on the other side.

THE COPING CODE: COPING WITH GRIEF DUE TO FAILURE IN EXAMINATION OR COURSE

Maximum Period of Sadness: 3 Months

> *"It is not the strongest of the species that survive, nor the most intelligent, but the one most responsive to change."*
> **– Charles Darwin**

Facing a failure, especially in something as significant as an examination or a course, can feel like a blow to your identity and self-worth. It's easy to feel as though all your efforts have been in vain, and the road ahead can seem uncertain. However, it's important to remember that failure is not the end but merely a stepping stone in the journey toward success. Everyone, no matter how successful, experiences setbacks and obstacles along the way. The key is how you respond to them.

Grieving a failure is a natural part of the process, and it can be helpful to understand that it's not about the failure itself but the feelings it brings up: disappointment, self-doubt, and perhaps frustration at not meeting expectations. You have the power to turn this setback into an opportunity for growth and improvement.

Samantha had always been a dedicated student. She spent long hours studying for her final exam in a course that was critical for her graduation. She had put in all the effort, reading every chapter, attending every review session, and practicing problems until her eyes hurt. But when the results were posted, Samantha was crushed to see that she had failed the exam. Her heart sank, and she immediately felt a wave of shame and disappointment.

"How could I fail?" she thought. "I worked so hard. What went wrong?"

For the next few days, Samantha isolated herself. She couldn't stop thinking about her failure and the disappointment she felt, not just for herself, but for her family, who had high expectations of her. She kept questioning where she went wrong and whether she was even cut out for this field.

Samantha's sadness was all-consuming, but she knew deep down that she needed to face it. She gave herself time to grieve, acknowledging that the sadness was valid. She reached out to her friend, Emily, who had been through a similar situation. Emily reminded Samantha that one exam, no matter how important, didn't define her worth.

"I felt just like you when I failed my exam," Emily said. "But it didn't stop me. It only made me more determined to figure out how to improve."

Samantha realized that Emily was right. She couldn't change what had happened, but she could learn from it. She took a few weeks to reflect on her study habits, identifying areas where she could improve. Rather than focusing on the failure itself, she decided to see it as a lesson that would make her stronger.

She reached out to her professor for feedback and revised her study plan. She also started practicing self-compassion, reminding herself that it was okay to fail. Everyone experiences setbacks, and this was just one moment in a much larger journey.

Samantha spent the next few months working hard, but with a renewed sense of purpose. She eventually retook the exam and passed with flying colours. The failure had allowed her to reassess her approach to studying, and she had come out of it stronger and more resilient.

While she would never forget how she felt during those painful moments, Samantha knew that failure wasn't the end of her story. It was simply the beginning of a new chapter.

Tips for Coping with Grief Due to Failure in Examination or Course

1. Acknowledge Your Emotions

Failure often brings a flood of emotions: disappointment, anger, frustration, and even embarrassment. It's important to allow yourself to feel these emotions instead of suppressing them.

Tip: Take time to sit with your emotions without judgment. Feeling sad or upset is normal and part of the grieving process. Allow yourself the space to feel what you're feeling.

2. Permit Yourself to Grieve

It's easy to push past grief, thinking you need to "move on" quickly. But grieving a failure is necessary to understand and learn from the experience.

Tip: Allow yourself time to process the failure. Whether it's a day or a week, take time to acknowledge your feelings, but also recognize that this sadness won't last forever.

3. Reflect, Don't Ruminate

It's natural to look back and analyse what went wrong. However, it's important to do this in a productive way. Reflecting can help you understand where things went wrong, but rumination—getting stuck in endless loops of regret and self-blame—will only hold you back.

Tip: Identify what you could have done differently, and then let go of the need to keep replaying the situation. Focus on what you can control moving forward.

4. Focus on the Bigger Picture

A failure in an exam or course does not define you as a person or as a student. One setback is not the totality of your future. Remember that this is just a chapter in your life, not the whole story.

Tip: Take a step back and see the bigger picture. One failure is not the end of your journey—it's just a temporary setback.

5. Reach Out for Support

Talking to someone who understands your feelings can be incredibly helpful. Whether it's a family member, friend, or counsellor, discussing your grief can offer comfort and perspective.

Tip: Don't isolate yourself. Talk to someone you trust. Sometimes, expressing your feelings aloud can bring clarity and relief.

6. Learn from the Experience

Failures often hold the best lessons. Use the time after your disappointment to reflect on what went wrong and how you can improve in the future.

Tip: View failure as a learning opportunity. Ask yourself: What did I learn from this experience? How can I apply this knowledge going forward?

7. Set New Goals

Once you've given yourself time to grieve, it's important to set new, realistic goals. This helps you move forward and regain focus. You may need to revise your study plan or find new methods of learning, but setting specific goals will help you stay motivated.

Tip: Break down your goals into smaller, manageable steps. This will help you regain a sense of control and purpose as you work toward your next success.

8. Practice Self-Compassion

It's easy to be hard on yourself when you fail, but being self-critical only adds to the pain. Treat yourself with the same kindness you would offer to a friend in a similar situation.

Tip: Remind yourself that everyone faces setbacks. Be kind to yourself, and avoid harsh self-judgment. You are doing your best.

9. Take Care of Your Physical Health

Grief and sadness can have an impact on your physical well-being. Exercise, sleep, and healthy eating play a crucial role in how we process emotions and handle stress.

Tip: Make time for physical activity, whether it's a walk, a run, or yoga. Taking care of your body will help you manage your emotions and improve your overall outlook.

10. Stay Open to New Opportunities

Failure can create an opportunity for new paths to open up. Use this time to think about alternative courses, certifications, or career paths you might not have considered before.

Tip: Keep an open mind and stay flexible. This setback might be an opportunity to explore new directions you hadn't thought of.

Failure in exams or courses can be a devastating blow, but it's important to remember that setbacks are part of life. With time, reflection, and a commitment to learning from the experience, you can overcome your grief and turn this moment of failure into an opportunity for growth.

THE COPING CODE: COPING WITH GRIEF DUE TO TROUBLE WITH YOUR BOSS

Maximum Period of Sadness: 3 Months

> *"It's not the situation, but how you react to the situation that matters."*
>
> **– Epictetus**

Having trouble with your boss can be an emotionally exhausting experience. Whether it's an ongoing conflict, misunderstandings, unfair treatment, or simply a difficult working relationship, the emotional toll can be heavy. It's not uncommon to feel powerless, frustrated, or even demoralized when you feel like you're at odds with someone who holds significant authority in your professional life. This kind of workplace tension can impact your confidence, productivity, and overall happiness.

However, the key to navigating such situations is understanding that you have the ability to control how you react, even if you can't control the actions of your boss. Recognizing your feelings, setting boundaries, and finding constructive ways to cope can help you move forward in a healthy way.

Jessica had been working as a project manager at a mid-sized company for over three years. She loved her job and had always been praised for her organizational skills and ability to meet deadlines. However, recently, her relationship with her boss, Mr. Thomas, had started to deteriorate.

At first, it was small things—miscommunications about project goals and increasing pressure to meet unrealistic deadlines. But as time went on, it escalated. Mr. Thomas began to micromanage every aspect of her work, questioning her decisions and undermining her confidence. His behaviour started to make Jessica feel anxious every time she entered the office.

One morning, after yet another tense meeting, Jessica sat at her desk, overwhelmed by a wave of sadness. She couldn't shake the feeling that no matter how hard she worked, it would never be good enough. She began doubting her abilities, feeling frustrated, and even considering quitting her job.

But Jessica knew she couldn't let this situation define her. After taking some time to reflect, she realized that the conflict wasn't entirely her fault. She had been doing her best, but the communication breakdown was at the root of the problem. She decided to have an honest conversation with Mr. Thomas to address their issues directly.

In their meeting, Jessica calmly explained how she felt about the constant micromanagement and lack of clarity in their communication. She requested more autonomy in her projects and asked for clearer expectations moving forward. Mr. Thomas was initially defensive, but after hearing her concerns, he softened and acknowledged that the pressure he was under might have contributed to his behaviour.

They agreed on a new approach to working together, with more open communication and mutual respect. While Jessica was relieved to have cleared the air, it wasn't a perfect solution. It took time for the relationship to fully improve, but the effort was worth it. Over the next few months, Jessica focused on maintaining professionalism, setting clear boundaries, and being proactive in her communication.

She also began practicing stress-relief techniques, like yoga and journaling, to manage the anxiety that had been building up. Slowly but surely, her emotional well-being improved. Jessica realized that, while the situation wasn't ideal, she had the power to control her reactions and work toward a resolution.

Months later, she had regained her confidence and felt much more at peace with the situation. She realized that even in a challenging work environment, she could maintain her dignity and emotional health. She learned that sometimes, the most important thing you can do is communicate honestly and take care of yourself, regardless of the challenges that come your way.

Tips for Coping with Grief Due to Trouble with Your Boss

1. Acknowledge Your Emotions

Recognizing your feelings is the first step toward dealing with them. You might feel upset, angry, or even defeated. It's important to acknowledge these emotions instead of burying them.

Tip: Take time to process your emotions and validate how you feel. Acknowledging your pain is the first step in healing.

2. Identify the Source of the Conflict

Understanding why the conflict exists can give you a clearer perspective on how to address it. Whether it's poor communication, mismatched expectations, or a difference in working styles, pinpointing the cause of the tension is crucial.

Tip: Reflect on what specifically is causing the issue. Is it something that can be resolved, or is it a deeper, ongoing issue? Knowing the root of the problem can help you decide the best course of action.

3. Keep Your Professionalism Intact

Even in challenging situations, maintaining your professionalism is key. Avoid engaging in gossip or letting your frustration show in your behaviour.

Tip: Stay focused on your work and maintain a level of professionalism, regardless of how you're feeling. Keeping a positive and productive attitude will not only reflect well on you, but it will also help you feel more in control.

4. Establish Boundaries

If your boss's behaviour is affecting your well-being, it may be necessary to establish healthy boundaries. This might mean limiting personal interactions or ensuring that work communications remain respectful and constructive.

Tip: Set clear boundaries for yourself regarding communication and interactions. You deserve to feel respected and valued, both as an employee and as a person.

5. Seek Clarification and Feedback

Misunderstandings can sometimes be the cause of conflict. Having an open and honest conversation with your boss may help clear up any confusion. Seek feedback on your performance and ask for specific guidance on how you can improve.

Tip: Approach the situation calmly and ask for constructive feedback. This will help you gain clarity and demonstrate your willingness to improve.

6. Talk to a Trusted Colleague or Mentor

Sometimes, having an outside perspective can provide insight into your situation. Talking to a trusted colleague or mentor about the conflict can help you see things from a different angle and receive valuable advice on how to handle the situation.

Tip: Confide in someone you trust. They may be able to offer a fresh perspective or suggest strategies for resolving the conflict.

7. Focus on What You Can Control

While you can't control your boss's behaviour, you can control your reaction. Focus on areas where you have influence and work to improve aspects of your work that can make you feel more empowered.

Tip: Shift your focus to things that are within your control, such as your performance and attitude. Small wins will help you regain confidence and feel less powerless.

8. Consider the Bigger Picture

Take a step back and look at the broader context of your job and career. Sometimes, workplace conflicts arise due to external pressures, not just personal differences. It may help to consider if the issue with your boss is temporary or related to bigger organizational challenges.

Tip: Step back and consider whether the problem is a temporary situation or part of a larger trend. Knowing this can help you decide how to move forward.

9. Practice Stress-Relief Techniques

The emotional toll of a difficult work environment can lead to stress and burnout. Incorporate stress-relief practices, such as exercise, meditation, or deep breathing, into your routine to help you manage your emotions and maintain your well-being.

Tip: Engage in activities that help you decompress. Whether it's going for a walk, doing yoga, or listening to calming music, find ways to unwind and release tension.

10. Decide When It's Time to Move On

Sometimes, no matter how much you try, the conflict with your boss may not improve. In such cases, it might be time to consider whether this job is still the right fit for you. If the environment becomes too toxic or unsupportive, it may be best to start looking for new opportunities.

Tip: If the situation doesn't improve despite your best efforts, it might be time to reassess your position. Consider whether a different job or work environment would allow you to thrive.

Having trouble with your boss is a challenging experience, but it doesn't have to be a roadblock. With patience, self-reflection, and a proactive approach, you can work through the conflict and regain your peace of mind. Remember, you are in control of how you respond, and your emotional well-being is always worth fighting for.

THE COPING CODE: COPING WITH GRIEF DUE TO CHANGE IN WORKING HOURS OR CONDITIONS

Maximum Period of Sadness: 3 Months

"The only way to make sense out of change is to plunge into it, move with it, and join the dance."

– **Alan Watts**

Changes in your working hours or conditions can create a profound sense of loss, frustration, or stress, especially if they disrupt your established routines. Whether you've been assigned a new shift, asked to work longer hours, or face new workplace expectations, these adjustments can bring about feelings of sadness and anxiety. Your emotional reaction is valid, and it's important to acknowledge and process these feelings. The good news is that, while the sadness may feel overwhelming at first, with time and a thoughtful approach, you can navigate this transition and even come out stronger.

The Coping Code: Coping With Grief Due to Change in Working Hours Or Conditions

Change is difficult, especially when it disrupts your sense of stability and personal life. However, how you approach this new phase is crucial in determining how long the sadness will last. In this chapter, we'll explore strategies to help you cope with changes in your working hours or conditions, with an emphasis on resilience and self-care.

Zoe had worked as a marketing manager at a fast-growing tech company for four years. She loved her job and was used to the steady routine of working from 9 AM to 5 PM. However, one day, Zoe was informed by her boss that the company was shifting to a new system of staggered shifts to accommodate growing client demands. Zoe was now required to work from 12 PM to 8 PM, which disrupted not only her work-life balance but also her sense of stability.

At first, Zoe was in shock. Her whole routine was built around her mornings. She loved having breakfast with her kids and spending time with her partner in the evenings. Now, everything felt upside down. She found herself feeling upset, frustrated, and, most of all, sad. The adjustment was hard, and she found herself withdrawing from her usual activities.

Her sadness intensified over the first couple of weeks. She struggled with insomnia due to the late hours and felt increasingly isolated from her family. The emotional toll of the change made it hard for her to focus at work, and she felt exhausted both mentally and physically.

After a month, Zoe realized that her current approach wasn't helping her feel better. She decided to take action. The first thing she did was have an open conversation with her supervisor about her feelings. She expressed how the shift change was affecting her personal life and asked if there was any way to adjust her schedule slightly to accommodate her needs. Her supervisor was empathetic and offered a solution by allowing her to have more flexible hours for certain days of the week.

Zoe also started adjusting her schedule. She set aside time in the mornings to exercise, which helped reduce her stress levels. On weekends, she made it a priority to spend quality time with her family, so she didn't feel so disconnected from them.

Zoe began to see small improvements. She started adjusting to her new work schedule and found that the flexibility her boss offered helped balance her personal life. She also started taking lunch breaks outside of the office to reconnect with her colleagues and alleviate the feeling of being isolated. Over time, she learned to embrace the changes, and her sadness began to fade.

Three months later, Zoe looked back and realized how much she had grown. She had successfully navigated the grief that came with the change and turned it into an opportunity for growth. She was now able to balance her career and personal life in a way that was better than before.

Tips for Coping with Grief Due to a Change in Working Hours or Conditions

1. Allow Yourself to Grieve

It's natural to feel upset when something disrupts your routine. Permit yourself to feel frustrated, sad, or even angry about the changes. Bottling up your emotions can make them harder to deal with later.

Tip: Take time to process your feelings. Acknowledge the loss of your previous routine and the impact of these changes on your life.

2. Identify What You're Losing and Gaining

Understanding both the positives and negatives of the change can help shift your perspective. While it may be uncomfortable, there might be benefits or opportunities that you hadn't initially noticed.

Tip: Make a list of both the pros and cons of the new work situation. This can help you evaluate the situation more objectively and find some silver linings.

3. Find Support

Talking to friends, family members, or colleagues who understand your situation can provide a sense of comfort. Knowing you're not alone in facing change can be reassuring.

Tip: Share your feelings with someone you trust. Sometimes, just talking it out can help you feel supported and understood.

4. Focus on What You Can Control

Change often feels overwhelming because it can make you feel like you've lost control. However, you can still control how you react and the adjustments you make in your personal life.

Tip: Focus on small things you can control, such as how you manage your time, your attitude toward the change, and the steps you take to make the transition smoother.

5. Establish a New Routine

One of the biggest challenges with changes in working hours or conditions is the disruption to your personal schedule. Creating a new routine can help you regain a sense of stability.

Tip: Try setting a daily routine that works with your new hours. This can help you feel more organized and reduce feelings of chaos.

6. Take Care of Your Physical Health

Stress can take a physical toll on your body. Make sure you're prioritizing self-care, including adequate rest, regular exercise, and a balanced diet to help you manage the stress of the transition.

Tip: Incorporate physical activities like yoga or walking into your day to alleviate stress. Exercise can boost your mood and improve your ability to cope with changes.

7. Set Boundaries with Work and Personal Life

With changes in working hours, it's easy for work to spill over into personal time. However, it's important to set boundaries to avoid burnout.

Tip: Be mindful of your time. If your new work conditions impact your work-life balance, set clear boundaries to ensure you still have time for relaxation and family.

8. Seek Professional Help if Needed

If your grief or sadness persists and becomes overwhelming, it might be helpful to talk to a counsellor or therapist who can assist you in healthily managing these emotions.

Tip: If you find that the sadness is hindering your daily life, don't hesitate to seek professional support. A therapist can provide strategies to cope with these challenges effectively.

9. Stay Flexible and Open to New Opportunities

Although change can be difficult, it often leads to new opportunities. Stay open to learning new skills or embracing the benefits of the change, even if they aren't immediately apparent.

Tip: Be open to new experiences that might come with your new work schedule or conditions. This can provide a sense of growth and excitement, even in the face of adversity.

10. Give It Time

Grief and adjustment take time. Be patient with yourself. It's normal to feel disoriented and sad at first, but with time, you'll adapt. It's important not to rush through the process.

Tip: Give yourself at least a few months to adjust to the changes. It's okay if things aren't perfect immediately.

Coping with grief due to changes in working hours or conditions is not easy, but it is manageable. By acknowledging your emotions, seeking support, focusing on what you can control, and making time for self-care, you can navigate this transition with resilience. Remember, it takes time to adjust, but with patience and proactive steps, you will adapt to the new changes and emerge even stronger.

THE COPING CODE: UNDERSTANDING AND PREVENTING SUICIDE: SUPPORTING LOVED ONES THROUGH THE DARKEST TIMES

"The greatest glory in living lies not in never falling, but in rising every time we fall."

— **Nelson Mandela**

Suicide is one of the most tragic outcomes of mental and emotional distress, and it often strikes when least expected. Tragically, those who seem to have it all – fame, fortune, success – are sometimes the ones who suffer most. It's important to recognize that no matter how much we may seem to have, we are all vulnerable to pain, suffering, and moments of hopelessness. In fact, it's often the high expectations and pressures of living in the spotlight that can make a person feel more isolated, even when surrounded by millions

Suicide is death caused by injuring oneself with the intent to die. A suicide attempt is when someone harms themselves with any intent to end their life, but they do not die as a result of their actions.

According to World Health Organisation, every year 703 000 people take their own life and there are many more people who attempt suicide. Every suicide is a tragedy that affects families, communities and entire countries and has long-lasting effects on the people left behind. Suicide occurs throughout the lifespan and was the fourth leading cause of death among 15–29-year-olds globally in 2019.

Suicide does not just occur in high-income countries, but is a global phenomenon in all regions of the world. In fact, over 77% of global suicides occurred in low- and middle-income countries in 2019.

Suicide is a serious public health problem; however, suicides are preventable with timely, evidence-based and often low-cost interventions. For national responses to be effective, a comprehensive multisectoral suicide prevention strategy is needed.

It's essential to understand that while animals in the wild don't commit suicide, human beings, as social animals, are prone to intense emotional and mental struggles, often resulting from overwhelming societal pressures. Unlike animals, humans have the capacity for complex emotional suffering, and it is sometimes this very ability to reflect and ponder that leads us down a darker path. But there is hope, and with the right support and coping mechanisms, those struggling with suicidal thoughts can find a way back to the light.

In this chapter, we'll look at the tragic suicides of some celebrities, each of whom had the world at their feet, yet struggled with inner turmoil. These stories, while heartbreaking, can teach us valuable lessons about the dangers of neglecting mental health and the importance of being vigilant for warning signs in ourselves and others.

Some Famous Celebrities Who Took Their Own Lives Despite Having Everything

1. Robin Williams (1951–2014)

Robin Williams was one of the most beloved actors and comedians of all time. His infectious laughter and ability to make others smile made him a global icon. Yet, behind his laughter, Williams struggled with depression and addiction. After a long battle, Williams took his own life in 2014, shocking the world. It was later revealed that he had been suffering from Lewy body dementia, a degenerative neurological disease that can cause severe depression, hallucinations, and cognitive decline.

2. Kurt Cobain (1967–1994)

Kurt Cobain, the lead singer of Nirvana, revolutionized the music industry with his raw and powerful sound. Despite his fame, Cobain struggled with addiction, depression, and a sense of alienation. At the age of 27, he took his own life in his Seattle home, leaving behind a legacy of music that still resonates with generations. Cobain's suicide shed light on the hidden struggles of fame and the isolation that often comes with it.

3. Chester Bennington (1976–2017)

Chester Bennington, the lead vocalist of Linkin Park, was known for his emotional and intense performances. He faced his own battles with depression, substance abuse, and the trauma of losing his close friend, Chris Cornell, to suicide just a few months before his own death. In 2017, Bennington died by suicide at the age of 41. His passing was a heartbreaking reminder of how even the strongest of us can be silently suffering.

4. Anthony Bourdain (1956–2018)

Anthony Bourdain was an internationally acclaimed chef, author, and television host. He travelled the world, sharing stories of food, culture, and human connection. Yet, despite his public persona as an adventurer and storyteller, Bourdain struggled with depression and addiction. His suicide in 2018, while in France filming an episode of his show, stunned his fans and loved ones. He was open about his mental health struggles in interviews, but many never realized the depth of his pain until it was too late.

5. Kate Spade (1962–2018)

Kate Spade was a fashion icon who built a multi-million-dollar brand around her designs. Her death by suicide in 2018 shocked the fashion world, especially as she had appeared in public just days before, seemingly happy and engaged with her work. Spade had been struggling with anxiety and depression, and her tragic passing highlighted how even those who appear successful and happy on the outside can be battling intense inner turmoil.

Stigma and taboo

Stigma, particularly surrounding mental disorders and suicide, means many people thinking of taking their own life or who have attempted suicide are not seeking help and are therefore not getting the help they need. The prevention of suicide has not been adequately addressed due to a lack of awareness of suicide as a major public health problem and the taboo in many societies to openly discuss it. To date, only a few countries have included suicide prevention among their health priorities and only thirty-eight countries report having a national suicide prevention strategy.

Raising community awareness and breaking down the taboo is important for countries to make progress in preventing suicide.

How to Prevent Suicidal Thoughts: Warning Signs, Symptoms, and Support

Suicidal thoughts can sometimes be a silent battle. The people closest to us may not outwardly show signs of distress, or may even mask their pain with smiles and laughter. Here are some key tips for preventing suicidal thoughts and offering support to those in need:

1. Be Aware of the Warning Signs

Understanding the warning signs of suicidal thoughts is crucial. While each person may exhibit different symptoms, there are common behaviours that may indicate someone is struggling:

- Talking about feeling hopeless or having no reason to live
- Talking about wanting to die or harm themselves
- Withdrawing from social interactions and activities
- Mood swings or extreme emotional distress
- Excessive alcohol or drug use
- Changes in behaviour, such as reckless behaviour or giving away possessions
- Expressing feelings of being a burden to others

2. Encourage Open Conversations

Sometimes, people suffering from suicidal thoughts may not feel comfortable speaking up. Be open to having difficult conversations with those you care about. Approach the subject with sensitivity and understanding. You don't have to have all the answers, but showing that you care can help the person feel less isolated.

- **Ask how they are really feeling.** Use open-ended questions, such as "How have you been doing lately?" or "I've noticed you seem down lately—what's going on?"
- **Listen attentively.** Avoid offering quick solutions or dismissing their feelings. Sometimes, simply listening can make a huge difference.

3. Encourage Professional Help

If someone expresses suicidal thoughts or you are concerned for their safety, encourage them to seek professional help. Therapy or counselling can provide the support needed to work through feelings of hopelessness and despair.

- **Help them find a mental health professional** or accompany them to an appointment if they're feeling uncertain about seeking help.
- **Don't minimize their feelings.** Let them know that it's okay to seek help and that doing so is a sign of strength, not weakness.

4. Be Supportive, But Set Boundaries

While it's important to offer emotional support, it's also crucial to encourage professional help. Being a support system for someone struggling with suicidal thoughts doesn't mean you should take on the role of their therapist. Encourage them to speak to a professional and provide resources if necessary.

- **Provide them with emergency resources**, such as the Suicide Prevention Lifeline.
- **Know when to call for help.** If you believe someone is in immediate danger, don't hesitate to contact emergency services.

5. Take Care of Yourself

Supporting someone through a crisis can take a toll on your emotional well-being. Don't neglect your own mental health. Seek support for yourself, whether it's talking to a trusted friend, counsellor, or support group.

How to Be a Support System for Those Struggling with Suicidal Thoughts

- **Offer empathy and understanding.** People struggling with suicidal thoughts often feel like no one understands them. Acknowledge their pain and offer a non-judgmental space for them to express themselves.
- **Be patient and persistent.** Suicidal thoughts may not disappear overnight, but with your ongoing support, they can begin to feel less overwhelmed. Check in with them regularly, even if they seem to be doing better.
- **Support their efforts in seeking help.** Encouraging them to attend therapy or take part in self-care activities shows that you're invested in their well-being.

The stories of celebrities like Robin Williams, Kurt Cobain, Chester Bennington, Anthony Bourdain, and Kate Spade remind us that no one is immune to the struggles of mental health. Success and fame cannot shield us from the battles we face internally. As friends, family, and support systems, it's essential to be vigilant for the warning signs, offer understanding, and encourage professional help.

Remember, suicide is preventable, and while the road to healing can be long, reaching out for support, taking action, and building connections can help save lives. It's important to recognize that no one should have to face their darkest moments alone. By supporting each other, we can create a world where mental health struggles are met with compassion, understanding, and hope.

> *"It's okay to not be okay, as long as you are not giving up."*
> **– Karen Salmonson**

SUICIDE PREVENTION HELPLINE

*S*uicide prevention helplines are critical resources for those in need of support, and many countries have dedicated numbers. Here's information on the suicide prevention helplines of some countries:

1. **United States**

- **National Suicide Prevention Lifeline**

Phone Number: 988 (24/7 helpline)

Website: www.suicidepreventionlifeline.org

2. **China**

- **China Suicide Prevention Helpline**

Phone Number: 800-810-1117 (Available 9 AM - 9 PM)

Website: www.chinahelpline.org

3. **India**

- **National Helpline for Suicide Prevention**

Phone Number: 91-22-2772 6771 or **91-22-2772 6773**

Website: www.suicidepreventionindia.org

- **Kiran Helpline (Mental Health Support)**

Phone Number: **1800-599-0019** (9 AM - 9 PM)

4. Russia

- **Russian Suicide Prevention Helpline**

Phone Number: **+7 495 626 36 36** (24/7 helpline)

Website: www.telefon-doveria.ru

5. Japan

- **TELL Lifeline (English-speaking)**

Phone Number: **03-5774-0992** (24/7)

Website: www.telljp.com
- **Tokyo Mental Health Crisis Helpline**

Phone Number: **03-5774-0992**

6. Germany

- **Telefonseelsorge (Telephone Counseling)**

Phone Number: **0800 111 0 111** or **0800 111 0 222** (24/7)

Website: www.telefonseelsorge.de

7. United Kingdom

- **Samaritans**

Phone Number: **116 123** (24/7 helpline)

Website: www.samaritans.org

8. France

- **SOS Suicide**

Phone Number: **01 45 39 40 00** (24/7 helpline)

Website: www.sos-suicide.org

9. Brazil

- **CVV (Centro de Valorização da Vida)**

Phone Number: **188** (24/7 helpline)

Website: www.cvv.org.br

10. Canada

- **Crisis Services Canada**

Phone Number: **1-833-456-4566** (24/7 helpline)

Text Support: Text **45645**

Website: www.crisisservicescanada.ca

These countries have dedicated national or regional suicide prevention services that operate 24/7, and most provide either phone or text-based support. Always reach out for help if you or someone you know is struggling with mental health or thoughts of self-harm.

www.ingramcontent.com/pod-product-compliance
Lightning Source LLC
LaVergne TN
LVHW041951070526
838199LV00051BA/2982